AF608081

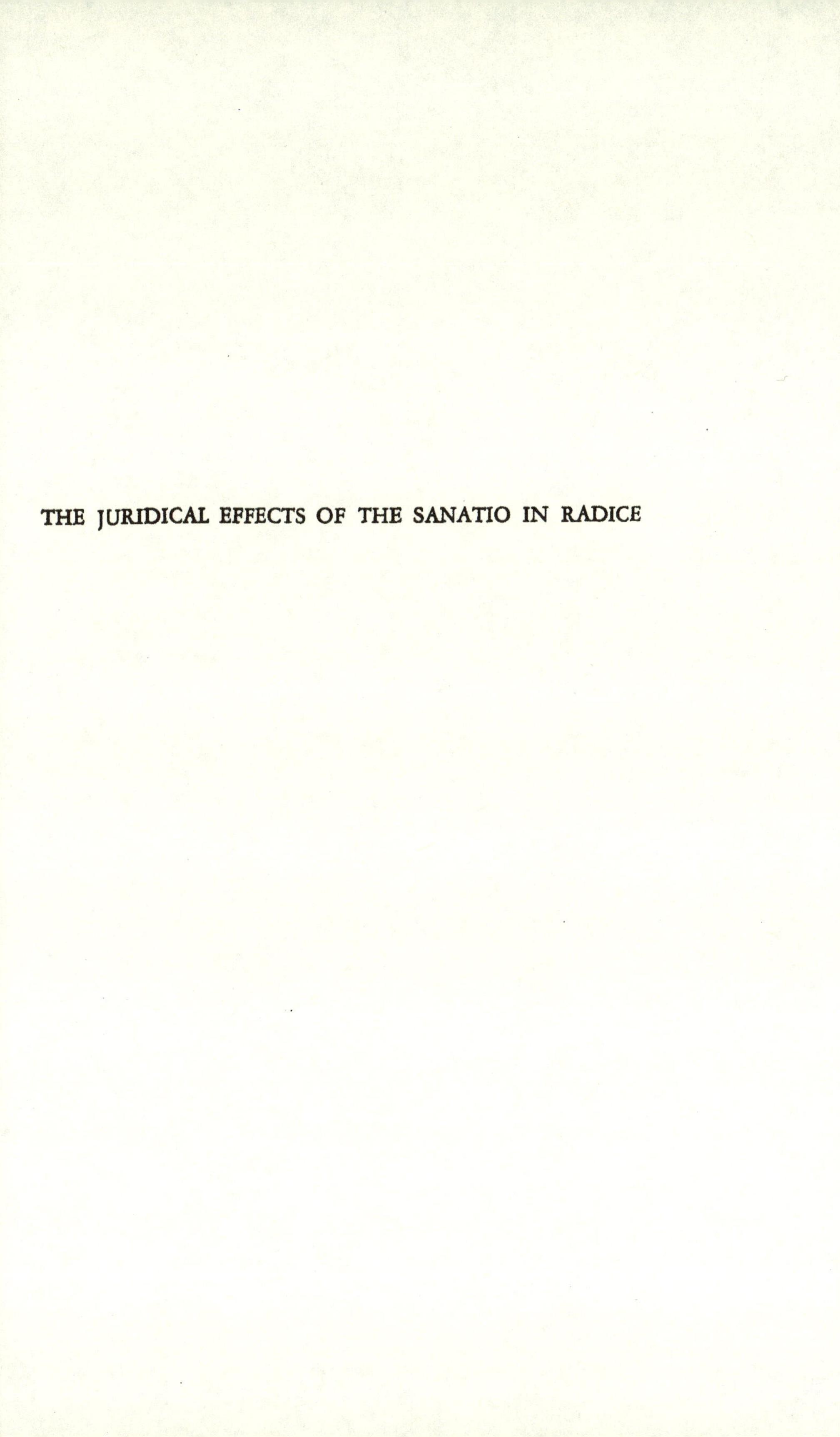

THE JURIDICAL EFFECTS OF THE SANATIO IN RADICE

uridical Effects of the Sanatio in Rac

A HISTORICAL SYNOPSIS AND A COMMENTARY

A DISSERTATION

BMITTED TO THE FACULTY OF THE SCHOOL OF CANON LAW OF THE CATHOLIC UNIVERSITY OF AMERICA IN PARTIAL FULFILLMENT OF THE REQUIREMENTS FOR THR DEGREE OF DOCTOR OF CANON LAW

BY

REV. THOMAS CHARLES RYAN, J.C.L.

PRIEST OF THE DIOCESE OF TRENTON

THE CATHOLIC UNIVERSITY OF AMERICA PRESS

WASHINGTON, D. C.

NIHIL OBSTAT:

J. ROGG SCHMIDT, A.B., J.C.D.
Censor Deputatus

Washingtonii, D.C., die 10 Augustii 1954

IMPRIMATUR:

✠ GEORGIUS GULIEMUS AHR, S.T.D.
Episcopus Trentoniensis

Trentonii, die 13 Augustii 1954

Printed by Libertarian Press, Glen Gardner, N. J.

TABLE OF CONTENTS

PART II

CANONICAL COMMENTARY

INTRODUCTION

Down through the ages one of the more unfortunate, and for the most part insoluble, problems that has plagued mankind has been the suffering and punishment that the innocent have been forced to endure for the offences of the guilty. An exemplified aspect of this widespread difficulty is the hardship and ignominy that befalls the progeny of illicit union through no culpability of the offspring. In this regard the Catholic Church, being ever motivated by charity and mercy, has established, beyond the ordinary dispensations which serve to safeguard the sacrament of matrimony, an extraordinary matrimonial dispensation. This dispensation has as one of its effects the alleviation, in some measure, of the repugnant results of the problem mentioned above. This deliverance is effected through an extraordinary process of legitimation. The name of the extraordinary matrimonial dispensation is the *sanatio in radice.*

It will be the purpose of the writer in this study to treat the juridical effects of the *sanatio in radice* and the manner in which the canonical effects flow from the *sanatio.* The study is divided into two parts. The first part furnishes an historical synopsis regarding the *sanatio in radice,* in which the pre-Code development of radical sanation is treated. The second part offers a canonical commentary, in which the juridical effects of a radical sanation are considered individually. This latter part consists of a separate treatment of 1) the convalidation of the invalid union; 2) the dispensation from the impediment; 3) the dispensation from the law of the renewal of consent, and 4) the retroaction of canonical effects (legitimation) to the past.

In chapter V, article IV, the writer treats of legitimation in its fundamental concept. In so doing he classifies the various types of illegitimate offspring as adulterine, sacrilegious, incestuous and nefarious. By describing the illegitimate children in this manner the writer means that the offspring are the products of either an adulterous union, a sacrilegious union, an incestuous union or an incestuous union in the direct line of consanguinity respectively.

Sanation is employed by the Church in things other than the marriage contract. However, the writer in this study restricts himself solely to the *sanatio in radice* as a matrimonial dispensation.

The writer wishes to express his gratitude to the Most Reverend George W. Ahr, Bishop of Trenton, for the opportunity to pursue studies in the School of Canon Law at the Catholic University of America; to the Faculty of the School of Canon Law; to the contemporary members of the School of Canon Law; and to anyone who has in any manner aided in the preparation of this study.

PART I

HISTORICAL SYNOPSIS

CHAPTER I

PRELIMINARY NOTIONS

Although the subject matter of this study is "The Juridical Effects of *The Sanatio in Radice,*" the writer should think himself rather presumptous were he to attempt to divorce the effects of *sanatio in radice* from the *sanatio* itself; accordingly he deems it but fitting that in giving the historical background of the subject he first explain the notions inherent in the expression *sanatio in radice* in order that the treatment of the effects may thus be better understood.

Article I. Definition of Terms

Etymologically the expression *sanatio in radice* derives directly from the Latin (*sanare*—to heal, or *sanatio*—a healing, and *radix*—root or source) and literally means a healing in the root or source. Thus a *sanatio in radice* evinces the Church's power to heal a marriage at its source, the source of a marriage being the exchange of consent by the parties.[1]

Once the terms have been defined, and it has been shown how the validation of a marriage by a *sanatio in radice* functions, it will become evident how appropriate and self-explanatory this Latin terminology is.

The proper or real definition of a *sanatio in radice* is given in the first paragraph of canon 1138 of *The Codex Iuris Canonici,*[2] which states as follows: "The healing of a marriage *in radice* is its validation, involving, besides the dispensation or cessation of the impediment, a dispensation from the law requiring renewal of consent, and retroaction by fiction of law, as regards canonical effects, to the past."[3]

---

[1] Canon 1081, §1.—Marimonium facit partium consensus inter personas iure habiles legitime manifestatus; . . .

[2] Canon 1138, §1.—Matrimonii in radice sanatio est eiusdem convalidatio, secumferens, praeter dispensationem vel cessationem impedimenti, dispensationem a lege de renovando consensu et retrotractionem, per fictionem iuris, circa effectus canonicos ad praeteritum.

[3] Bouscaren and Ellis, *Canon Law—A Text and Commentary,* 2. ed., (2nd printing, Milwaukee: Bruce, 1953), p. 636 (Hereafter cited as *Canon Law.*).

The definition of *sanatio in radice* as found in *The Code of Canon Law* definitely points out that a *sanatio in radice* is primarily and essentially the validation of a hitherto invalid marriage. According to Canon Law,[4] an act is null when there is lacking in it that which essentially constitutes the act or when it is found wanting in those solemnities or conditions that are required by the sacred canons under pain of nullity. A marriage contract that is null may have its validity restored through one of two methods. The first method of validating a previously invalid marriage is called "simple convalidation."[5]

This is the common method of validating a previously invalid marriage and it is the ordinary procedure whenever it may be used. It is the second method which, comparatively speaking, is rarely used and is the extraordinary means of validating a marriage, that is the topic of this work; namely, the *sanatio in radice.*

Article II. Division of the *Sanatio in Radice*

A twofold division of the *sanatio in radice* may be made according to whether or not the convalidation carries with it the three additional effects mentioned in canon 1138, §1, in their entirety. The Code itself is silent as regards a division of radical sanation. However, most of the authors teach that a radical sanation is either perfect (total) or imperfect (partial), depending upon whether or not the convalidation is accompanied with the dispensation form the impediment, the dispensation from the law of the renewal of consent, and the retroaction of the canonical effects to the past.[6]

---

[4] Canon 1680, §1.

[5] Canons 1133-1337. Cf. *infra,* p. 76.

[6] Payen, *De Matrimonio in Missionibus* (3 vols., ZiKa-Wei, 1935-1936.), II, n. 2608; Harrigan, *The Radical Sanation of Invalid Marriages* (The Catholic University of America Canon Law Studies, n. 116, The Catholic University of America, Washington, D. C., 1938.), pp. 10-11 (hereafter cited as Harrigan.); Gasparri, *Tractatus Canonicus de Matrimonio* (2 vols., Nova ed., ad mentem Codicis, Romae: Typis Polyglottis Vaticanis, 1932), II, n. 1212 (hereafter referred to as *De Matrimonio*); Bouscaren-Ellis, *Canon Law,* p. 637; Chelodi-Ciprotti, *Ius Canonicum de Matrimonio* (5 ed., Vicenza: Società Anonima Tipografica Editrice, 1947), n. 167; Cappello, *Tractatus Canonico-Moralis de Sacramentis* (5 vols., Vol. IV *De Sacra Ordinatione,* 3 ed. Vol. V, *De Matrimonio,* 6 ed. Taurinorum Augustal: Marietti), *De Matrimonio,* n. 850,

Although the Code does not make any such division of radical sanation, the writer believes that the division is quite helpful in studying the *sanatio in radice*. The division of radical sanation emphasizes the various effects of sanation and thus is very advantageous in this study.

A perfect radical sanation is had if the convalidation of the invalid union is effected and this convalidation carries with it the juridical effects mentioned in canon 1138, §1, in their fullest measure. Should any of these juridical effects be wanting or not present in their fullest possible measure, the sanation cannot be perfect. Thus for a perfect sanation there must be effected 1) the convalidation of the invalid union; 2) the dispensation from the impediment that caused the invalidity of the union; 3) a dispensation from the law of the renewal of consent, and 4) the retroaction of the canonical effects, through a fiction of law, to the time that the invalid union was initially entered.

The fact that neither of the parties or just one of the parties be cognizant of the radical sanation[7] has no bearing upon whether the *sanatio* is perfect or imperfect. This depends entirely upon the convalidation and the completeness of the three additional effects that accompany the convalidation.[8]

Convalidation by radical sanation is imperfect if the convalidation does not carry with it all three of the juridical effects that are named in canon 1138, §1, or if one or more of these effects be not present in its fullest sense.

First, then, a convalidation by radical sanation may be imperfect because the convalidation does not carry with it a dispensation from the impediment that originally caused the invalidity of the union. Such a case would be had if the impediment that caused the invalidity of the union was the impediment of nonage. Thus, if John and Mary attempted to contract marriage on June 1, 1932, when both parties were

§4; Coronata, *De Sacramentis* (3 vols., 2. ed., Taurini: Marietti, 1943-1946), Vol. III, *De Matrimonio*, n. 684.

[7] Canon 1138, §3.

[8] Payen, *De Matrimonio in Missionibus*, II, p. 2608; Cappello, *De Sacramentis, V, De Matrimonio*, n. 850, §4 bis; Bouscaren-Ellis *Canon Law*, p. 637; Wernz-Vidal, *Ius Canonicum ad Codicis Norman Exactum* (7 vols. in 8, Vol. V, *Ius Matrimoniale*, 3. ed., Romae: Apud Aedes Universitatis Gregorianae, 1946), V *Ius Matrimoniale*, n. 659.

two years younger than the required canonical age, the marriage remained invalid for that reason.[9] However, if some six years later a *sanatio in radice* was sought for the marriage and was granted, that convalidation did not carry with it a dispensation from the impediment. The reason is that by the time the sanation was granted the impediment of nonage had already ceased. A dispensation cannot be given if there is nothing from which to dispense.

Secondly, a radical sanation may be imperfect because the convalidation does not carry with it a dispensation from the law of the renewal of consent. Such a situation would be present if one party were dispensed from the renewing of consent whereas a renewal of consent were demanded of the other party.[10] If consent is lacking in one of the parties for whom the sanation is sought, no convalidation can be given until the necessary consent is supplied, for no marriage can be effected without the mutual exchange of marital consent.[11]

Thirdly, and finally, a *sanatio in radice* may be imperfect because the retroaction of the canonical effects does not extend back to the inception of the union. A case of this nature would be had if consent were lacking on the part of one, or both, of the parties when they first entered their union. Then at some later point in the course of the union the true marital consent may be supplied. In this instance the retroaction extends back, not to the beginning of the union, but rather to the point in time at which a true marital consent was given.[12] The point of time at which the abiding true marital consent was first exchanged points to the *radix* of the union that is being sanated. It is the initial point of time in this *radix* that is the *terminus ad quem* for the reversion of the canonical effects through the fiction of law.[13]

In addition to the division of perfect and imperfect radical sanation there is also another division. This second division classifies sanations as being radical sanations properly socalled and radical sanations improperly socalled. A radical sanation properly socalled is effected

---

[9] Canon 1067.

[10] Payen, *De Matrimonio in Missionibus,* II, p. 2608, §2; Bouscaren-Ellis, *Canon Law,* p. 637.

[11] Canon 1081, §1.

[12] Canon 1140, §2.—Quod si consensus ab initio quidem defuerit, sed postea praestitus fuerit, sanatio concedi potest a momento praestiti consensus.

[13] Cf. *infra,* pp. 102 ff.

when the sanation involves the convalidation of the marriage in question. A radical sanation improperly socalled occurs when it is not a convalidation, but only the retroactive grant of the canonical effects that is effected. A radical sanation improperly socalled is had when one of the parties is deceased or perpetually insane. In this case no convalidation is possible, and hence only the retroactive grant of the canonical effects is made.[14]

---

[14] Payen, *De Matrimonio in Missionibus,* II, p. 2607.

CHAPTER II

A Historical Synopsis of the Sanatio in Radice

Either the *sanatio in radice* or any kindred dispensation did not exist during the first five centuries of the Christian era, or else the documents bearing proof thereof have vanished unknown to succeeding eras in the history of the Church. The sixth century brings to light for the first time, it would seem, the existence of such a dispensation in the legal repertory of the Church. Even in this instance, however, the historical reference is vague, and the following two nineteenth century scholars stand almost alone in asserting that the sixth century heralded the beginning of the *sanatio in radice.*

Article I. The View of Perrone and Giovine

The Jesuit, Giovanni Perrone (1794-1876), General Perfect of Studies in the Roman College, writing in the year 1858, initially expressed the opinion that the first recorded *sanatio in radice* was granted in the first half of the sixth century.[1] Perrone based his opinion on the legislation of the III Council of Orleans (538), which was in part concerned with the problems that confronted the Church upon the reception of converts to the True Faith. Many of these new Christians had before their conversion entered invalid marriages in the face of the diriment impediment of consanguinity and had thus involved themselves in incestuous unions. Many of these marriages were putatively good, since the involved parties entered the marriages in good faith, not being aware of the diriment impediment of consanguinity. The fathers of the Council, therefore, were reluctant to enact directly any legislation that would publicly brand these marriages as invalid, since such a pronouncement could quite conceivably have caused much more harm than good. The solution of the Council to this difficulty is found in canon 10 of the enactments of the Council. This canon decreed that the parties who though materially invalidly married, were in good faith should be allowed to remain that way. It further stated that their

---

[1] *De Matrimonio Christiano* (3 vols., Leodii, 1861), II, 163: Wernz-Vidal, *Ius Matrimoniale,* p. 862.

marriages should be regarded and treated as perfectly valid marriages, but that anyone who contracted marriage in the future, i.e., after the promulgation of the laws of the Council, would most certainly be bound by the laws regarding consanguinity.[2]

Perrone interpreted this canon as meaning that the Church was granting a tacit *sanatio in radice* to each of the invalid marriages contracted in good faith prior to the Council.[3] He even asks quite bluntly what else other than a *sanatio* could the Council have meant in Canon 10.[4]

Pietro Giovine, a contemporary of Perrone, wrote a scant five years (1863) after *De Matrimonio Christiano* appeared. His expressed view coincided almost to the letter with that of Perrone. Both writers were of the following opinion: 1) the Council did not leave the parties referred to above in good faith without any form of convalidation of the marriages; and 2) the Council did not believe that invincible ignorance excused from invalidating impediments. Rather, they held, that the Council sanated the invalid marriages at their roots, thus obviating the necessity of renewing consent and also granting retroactively all of the effects of valid marriages *ab initio* to these unions.[5]

"In addition to the III Council of Orleans which the above authors cited in confirming their views, there is found similar legislation in two earlier councils: Canon 61 of the Council of Agde (506),[6] and in

---

[2] Bruns, *Canones Apostolorum et Conciliorum Saeculorum IV-VII* (2 vols., Berolini, 1839), II, 194: Hardouin, *Acta Conciliorum et Epistolae Decretales ac Constitutiones Summorum Pontificum* (12 vols., Parisiis), II, 1425: Mansi, *Sacrorum Conciliorum Nova et Amplissima Collectio* (53 vols. in 60, Parisiis, 1901-1927), IX, 14 "De incestis coniunctionibus ita quae sunt statuta serventur, ut his qui aut modo ad baptismum veniunt, aut quibus patrum statuta sacerdotali praedicatione in notitiam non venerunt, ita pro novitate conversionis ac fidei suae credidimus consulendum, ut contracta huiusque huiusmodi coniugia non solvantur, sed in futurum quod de incestis coniuncionibus in anterioribus canonibus interdictum est observetur: id est, ut ne quis sibi sub nomine coniugii sociore praesumat relictam patris, filiam uxoris, relictam fratris, sororem uxoris, consobrinam, aut sobrinan, relictam avunculi vel patrui."

[3] Perrone, *De Matrimonio Christiano,* II, 163.

[4] *Loc. cit.*

[5] Giovine, *De Dispensationibus Matrimonialibus,* I, Consult. XXIII, Sect. 23, n. 7 as cited in Feije, *De Impedimentis et Dispensationibus Matrimonialibus,* (3. ed., Lovonii, 1885), p. 787 and Harrigan, pp. 20 ff.

[6] Hardouin, II, 1005: Mansi, VIII, 335: Bruns, II, 153.

Canon 30 of the Council of Epaon in Burgundy, which convened in the year 517.[7] The Fourth Council of Orleans (541) merely reiterated what the III Council had already enacted.[8]

The view espoused by Perrone and Giovine attracted very few adherents in the canonical world. If the sixth century did mark the first use of the *sanatio in radice,* then the historical data of the succeeding centuries fail to support this fact. It was not until the thirteenth century that canonists began to discuss the type of dispensation that today is termed radical sanation. And it was not until the beginning of the fourteenth century that the grant of the first radical sanation was actually recorded. In the following section a brief treatment will be given to the canonical thought that preceded the first actual grant of a radical sanation.

Article II. The Opinions of Medieval Canonists

There arose historical exigencies that called for the establishing of various media for the legitimating of children in order that rightful heirs might be constituted, families kept in being, *patria potestas* protected, and in general the continued survival of Roman society insured. Comparable to this was the need in the medieval period of the Church's history that called for a special favor from the Church for the obliteration of the infamy that attached to illicit progeny. Legitimate birth was a matter of great import, since illegitimacy barred a person from receiving civil office, from attaining to dignities, or from becoming an heir. Thus the legislation affecting legitimation was one of the prime matters discussed by authors at that time.[9]

The deep concern that scholars had for the problem of legitimation

---

[7] Bruns, II, 166: Mansi, VIII, 562-563: Hardouin, II, 1050: *Monumenta Germaniae Historica,* (mgh), Legum Sectio III, Concilia, Tom I, *Concilia Aevi Merovingici* (Resensuit Fredericus Maassin, Hannoverae, 1883) p. 25.

[8] Can. 27—Hardouin, III, 1437: Bruns, II, 206: *MGH,* Legum Sectio III, *Concilia,* Tom I, *Concilia Aevi Merovingici,* p. 93: Mansi, IX, 118.

[9] Panormitanus (Nicholaus de Tudeschis—1386—a. 1453) *Commentariain Quinque Libros Decretalium,* (5 vols. in 7, Venetiis, 1588), C. 13, X, *qui filii sint legitimi,* IV, 22 ff: Hostiensis (Henricus de Segusio, + 1271), *Summa Aurea,* (Venetiis, 1570), C. 13, X, tit. *qui filii sint legitimi;* St. Thomas Aquinas (1224-1274), *Summa Theologica* (*cum textu ex Recensione Leonina,* 3 vols., Taurini, Romae: Marietti 1949-1950), Supplementum, q. 68, Artt. 1, 2, 3.

stirred the contemporary canonists into attempting to determine just how the power of the papacy and this indirect legitimation could be reconciled. Five distinct opinions on this problem are to be found in the *Commentaria* of Panormitanus.[10]

Johannes Teutonicus (†1245) was of the view that the pope did not have power to grant legitimation regarding temporal things, but only in regard to spiritual things. However, since the spiritual order was definitely of a higher nature than the temporal order, naturally the higher included the lower, and so the pope could indirectly grant legitimation in regard to the temporal things.[11]

The early thirteenth century writers, Laurentius, Vincentius, and Tancredus, according to Panormitanus, concurred in the view that the pope could legitimate in respect to temporal things, but that this legitimation carried with it no civil effects. However, the three did add that the children legitimized were then free to seek temporalities that were only obtainable by legitimate persons.[12]

Bernardus de Botone (†1266) approached the problem in a different manner. He divorced the spiritual entirely from the temporal. Having done this, he concluded that ,whereas the pope could most certainly legitimize for spiritual things, he was incapable of legitimating for temporal offices.[13]

---

[10] C. 13, X, *qui filii sint legitimi,* IV, 22 ff.

[11] *Glossa,* ad c. 13, X, *qui filii sint legitimi,* IV, 17, s. v. habeat *potestatem:* "Ad hoc dixit Johannes quod dominus papa non habet potestatem legitimandi in temporalibus: sed, eo ipso quod legitimat aliquem quoad spiritualia, per consequens legitimat eum quoad temporalia quae sunt minus digna, et sic legitimat per consequentiam, sed non directe: saepe enim permittitur aliquid indirecte quod non permittitur directe."

[12] *Glossa,* ad c, 13, X, *qui filii sint legitimi,* IV, 17 s. v. *habeat potestatem;* "Tandem quidam extendunt legitimationem ad honores saeculares unde per hoc intelligitur legitimatus ut possit esse iudex et habere huius modi honores temporales quos alios habere non posset. Et in hac sententio fuerunt Laurentius, Vincentius et Tancredus."

[13] *Glossa,* ad c. 13, X, *qui filii sint legitimi,* IV, 17, s. v. *habeat potestatem:* "Propter hoc tamen legitimat quod aliquem in spiritualibus non probatur quod habeat iurisdictionem in temporalibus. Legitimare enim pertinet ad voluntarium iurisdictionem: item quia papam nihil spectat de temporalibus: et sic videtur quod papa quoad temporalia legitimare non possit ubi non habet iurisdictionem temporalem . . . Sed contrarium credo scilicet, quod dominus papa non potest legitimare aliquem quantum ad hoc ut succedat in hereditate, tamquam legitimus

The fourth opinion, as revealed by Panormitanus, was that of Hostiensis (Henricus de Segusio, d. 1271), famed Cardinal and author of the thirteenth century. Hostiensis varied from the three preceding views in that he was not immediately concerned with the effects, i.e., whether they be spiritual or temporal, of the pope's legitimating. Rather he took up the cause or source of the legitimacy, namely, a valid marriage, and began to work from there. The argument of Hostiensis ran along the following vein: that if the Church possessed the power to render a marriage invalid and, consequently, the children illegitimate by placing a diriment impediment to the marriage, then the Church logically also had the power to restore legitimacy to children who often were rendered illegitimate in consequence of the laws of the Church. Thus in restoring legitimacy to children, whether that legitimacy affected spiritual or temporal affairs, the Church assuredly remained within its own orbit of control, since it would be leading only with a marriage that admittedly lay within the scope of its Jurisdiction.[14]

The fifth and final view was that of Joannes Andreae (1270-1348), a very noted medieval canonist. According to Chelodi (1880-1922) his view was proposed near the middle of the fourteenth century.[15]

Joannes Andreae held that the pope could validate a previously invalid marriage, provided that the reason for the invalidity was a diriment impediment of the ecclesiastical law, and not of the divine law. Thus a marriage that was null in view of the degrees of affinity

---

haeres, qui non sit, dico, de sua iurisdictione temporali. Sic enim esset mittere falcem in messem alienam, et usurpare alienam iurisdictionem, quod esse non debet, et privare aliquem iure succedendi, unde credo quod non possit legitimare nisi quoad actus spirituales."

[14] Hostiensis, *Summa Aurea,* ad c. 13, *qui filii sint legitimi,* IV, 17, n. 11: "Salva reverentia aliorum, mihi videtur dominum papam habere potestatem legitimandi quoad spiritualia et temporalia et ipsum solum. . . . Sed papa vere legitimat et illegitimat. Cum enim secundum leges filii duorum fratrum rite contrahant et etiam secundum legem divinam quam iudaei servant, de fidelibus papa huiusmodi matrimonium legitimum fecit, et sic filii suscepti ex tali matrimonio hodie secundum legem et secundum canonem ab haereditate repelluntur. Multum enim personae prohibentur lege canonum con trahere quae lege divina on prohibentur. Si vero illegitimos facit, quanto magis poterit legitimare."

[15] Chelodi Ciprotti, *Ius Canonicum de Matrimonic,* p. 212.

or consanguinity which the Church had established as diriment impediments could be validated by the Holy Father. This validation reached back to the very moment the marriage began—*usque ad radicem*—and besides restoring validity to the marriage contract it also restored all of the effects proper to a true valid union.[16]

Thus since the effects of the valid marriage reverted to the instant of the entrance into matrimony by the parties, the children that were legitimated in this fashion enjoyed all of the canonical and civil rights, just as though they had been born of an originally valid marriage. This, then, meant that by the process the pope could not only legitimate as regards spiritual and temporal affairs in his own territory, but also that he could legitimate for temporal as well as spiritual affairs in lands other than his own.[17]

The view of Joannes Andreae truly then safeguarded the power of the papacy in regard to legitimating for temporal affairs in lands outside the papal temporal territory. Also this unfailing, if indirect, manner of legitimating so interwove the effects of the marriage with the marriage itself that, though the pope was dealing directly with the marriage only, simultaneously he treated indirectly and inevitably with the effects flowing from this marital union.[18]

Article III. First Recognized Grant of a Radical Sanation

Pope Boniface VIII (1294-1303) appears to have been the first pontiff to exercise the power to grant a *sanatio in radice*. Rigantius (1661-1735) was rather explicit about Boniface being the first to do this.[19] Rigantius did not give the exact date of this grant by Boniface VIII; he stated simply that it was made prior to 1305, the date of a grant of another [*sanatio in radice*] dispensation by Pope Clement V,[20]

---

16 Joannes Baptista Regantius, *Commentaria in Regulas, Constitutiones et Ordinationes Cancellariae Apostolicae, Opus Posthumum* (IV Vols., Coloniae Allobrogum, 1751) Tom. IV, Reg. L, n. 106 (hereafter cited as *Commentaria in Regulas*).

17 *Loc. cit.*

18 Panormitanus, *Commentaria,* ad c. 13, X, qui filii sint legitimi, IV, 17, nn. 26 ff.; Rigantius, *op. cit., Loc. cit.*

19 Rigantius, *op. cit.,* Tom. IV, Reg. XLIX, n. 11: ". . . quod fuit prima Dispensatio in radice Matrimonii quae concessa legitur."

20 Rigantius, *ibid.,* n. 10.

but other authors fix the date as being 1301.[21] The first *sanatio,* then, was granted perhaps some forty years before the view of Ioannes Andreae was presented to the canonical world.

The first recipient of this novel and greatly beneficial dispensation was Maria, widow of Sancius IV (1284-1296), deceased king of Castile, which made the first *sanatio* an imperfect one. The marriage had been invalid because Maria and Sancius were related in the third degree of consanguinity.[22]

Shortly after this Boniface VIII granted the first perfect *sanatio.* On this occasion the recipients of the dispensation were also involved in a union which was null owing to the impediment of consanguinity.[23]

These two grants, thought not necessarily the only two occasions on which a pope exercised his power to sanate a marriage at its roots, do appear to be the only two recorded uses of this papal power in the fourteenth and possibly fifteenth centuries.

Possibly, then, the period between the end of Boniface VIII's reign in 1303 and the convening of the Council of Trent in 1545 was unproductive of dispensations of this nature. And what grants there were, if any, were very few in number, as this type of validation was definitely a rarity prior to Tridentine Council.

Article IV. General Radical Sanations

The occasion for the employing of the first general *sanatio in radice* was the accumulation of complicated problems that faced the Holy See during the critical post-Reformation days of Queen Mary Tudor's reign (1553-1558). With a Catholic ruler once more seated upon the throne of England, the end of the "divorce" schism, begun by King Henry VIII (1509-1547) and intensified during the days of Edward VI's rule (1547-1553), was eagerly sought. Rome hopefully anticipated a complete return of Great Britain to the true Faith.

A solution for the many difficulties that existed during these troublesome days in England was decided upon in 1554. On St. Andrew's Day, Nov. 30, 1554, Reginald Cardinal Pole absolved the

[21] Chelodi, Ciprotti, *Ius Canonicum de Matrimonio,* p. 212: Wernz-Vidal, *Ius Matrimoniale,* p. 863: Cappello, *De Sacramentis,* V, *De Matrimonio,* n. 858.

[22] Rigantius, *op. cit.,* Tom. IV, Reg. XLIX, n. 10, 11.

[23] Rigantius, *op. cit., loc. cit.*

English people and received them back into union with Rome.[24] Although the obstacles with which the Holy See had to deal in bringing the English people back to Rome were numerous, the only one that is of concern here is the prolific marriage problem.

During the years of the rupture between the Holy See and England, a number of marriages were entered into within the prohibited degrees of consanguinity without benefit of a dispensation. As a result these marriages were invalid. In order to validate these marriages without having to perform the practically impossible task of ferreting out each invalidated marriage, Pope Julius III in 1554 granted a general *sanatio in radice* that sanated all of the marriages invalidly contracted in England during the schism because of the impediment of consanguinity. The parties living in these unions did not have to renew consent, but were to continue in their marriage as though no impediment had ever marred their union.[25]

The granting of this general *sanatio in radice* to England by Pope Julius III in 1554 was of far-reaching import not only because of the part it played in temporarily restoring England to union with the Holy See, but also because of the historical significance it had in the development of this type of dispensation. Prior to this the granting of sanations had been undertaken by the Holy See only for specific cases in individual instances.[26] The granting of this general *sanatio in radice* for England by Pope Julius III is the first recorded grant of a general favor of this kind.[27] Besides being the first general *sanatio in radice,* this grant by Pope Julius III was very important in the historical development of this type of marriage validation dispensation, for it indicated a change in emphasis as regards the effects flowing from a radical sanation. Prior to that time the chief concern relative to the effects of this ratification had to do with the legitimation of the

---

24 *Collectanea Sacrae Congregationis de Propaganda Fidei,* (2 vols., Romae, Typographia Polyglotta S. C. de Propaganda Fide, 1907), n. 1566.

25 Wernz, *Ius Decretalium* (6 vols., Vol. IV, Romae, 1904), IV, n. 654: Cappello, *De Sacramentis,* V *De Matrimonis,* n. 858: Haile, *The Life of Reginald Pole* (New York, 1910), p. 445: Harrigan, p. 31.

26 Rigantius, *Commentaria in Regulas,* Tom. IV, Reg. XLIV, nn. 10, 11.

27 Cappello, *De Sacramentis,* V, *De Martimoni,* p. 870; Wernz-Vidal, *Ius Matrimoniale,* p. 863, note 19.

offspring.[28] However, the situation as found in Tudor England caused to be stressed the fact previously obscured by the concern over the problem of legitimation; namely, that whether or not there were children to be legitimated, the *sanatio in radice* carried with it a validation of the marriage itself. Thus the granting of a *sanatio in radice* was important not only to the children because of the benefits derived from the dispensation, but to the parents as well because of the direct bearing it had upon the validation of their marriage.

The granting of the first recorded general *sanatio in radice* by Pope Julius III in 1554 opened the door, as it were, for future pontiffs to solve complex marriage problems of a similar nature by using the same means that Pope Julius III found so practical. In the remainder of this article the writer will endeavor to give a chronological schema, though by no means complete, of the more important grants of this nature that were made since the Council of Trent.

Pope Clement VIII (1592-1605) in the year 1595 granted a general *sanatio in radice* for the validation of a number of Greek marriages. These had been entered into invalidly because the married parties were within the fourth degree of consanguinity.[29]

The year 1644, the last year in the reign of Pope Urban VIII (1623-1644), witnessed the initiation of an important new development in the history of the *sanatio in radice.* This innovation consisted in the delegation issued to others by the Holy Father of the faculty of sanating marriages.

The grant was made through the Sacred Congregation for the Propagation of the Faith on February 28, 1644; the recipients were a group of French missioners.[30]

In the eighteenth century grants of the *sanatio in radice* became more numerous.[31] Pope Clement XI (1700-1721) effected a sanation on April 2, 1701, in his letter *Apostolicae Dignitatis.*[32] A third of a

---

[28] Hostiensis, *Summa Aurea,* ad c. 13, X, *qui filii sint legitimi,* IV, 17; St. Thomas Aquinas, *Summa Theologica,* Supplementum, q. 68, artt. 1, 2, 3.

[29] Cappello, *De Sacramentis,* V, *De Matrimonio,* n. 858.

[30] Perrone, *De Matrimonio Christiano,* II, 157.

[31] Chelodi-Ciprotti, *Ius Canonicum de Matrimonio,* p. 212.

[32] Benedictus XIV (Prospero Lambertini), *De Synodo Dioecesana* (2 ed., 4 vols., Mechliniae, 1842), Lib. XIII, c. XXI, n. 7: *Institutiones Ecclesiasticae* (3. ed., Latina Veneta, II vols., Venetiis, 1788) LXXXVIII, n. 80.

century later Pope Clement XII (1730-1740) on September 9, 1734, issued a bull, *cum dudum,* to the Provincial of the missionaries of the Society of Jesus laboring in the mission fields of the East Indies, in which bull he granted a general *sanatio in radice.*[33]

Pope Benedict XIV (1740-1758), the celebrated canonist Pope, succeeded Clement XII. Since, however, the writer intends to treat the present subject in the works of Benedict XIV at greater length elsewhere in this study, only a passing glance will now be given in his direction. Suffice it to observe here that in the *Institutiones Ecclesiasticae* and *De Synodo Dioecesana* of Benedict much may be learned concerning the use of the dispensation, *sanatio in radice* given by his predecessors.

Benedict's immediate successors, Pope Clement XIII (1758-1769) and Pope Pius VI (1775-1799), granted sanations for marriages in France that were invalid in consequence of the invalid granting of dispensations by various French bishops.[34] In connection with the pontificate of Pope Pius VI a noteworthy change in the use of terminology took place. The type of dispensation that is the subject of this study was not always termed a *sanatio in radice.*

From the time of Boniface VIII and his first grant of such a dispensation in 1301, however, there was little doubt, in view of the means used and the effects produced, that the various pontiffs were granting what today is generally termed a *sanatio in radice.* The term *sanatio in radice* appears to have been employed for the first time in the year 1788.[35] Prior to this date the usually employed expression was *dispensatio in radice.* Fifteen years later Cardinal Caprara in issuing his instruction to the bishops of France employed both terms,[36] a use which reflected the novel character of the term *sanatio in radice* on the one hand and the customary acceptance of *dispensatio in radice* on the other.

France likewise was the focal point for the granting of two general

---

33 *Magnum Bullarium Romanum* (19 vols. in 18, Luxemburgi, 1727-1754), XXIV, 5-8.

34 Perrone, *De Matrimonio Christiano,* II, 157.

35 *Codicis Iuris Canonici Fontes* (cura Emī. Petri Card. Gasparri editi., 9 vols., Romae (postea Civitate Vaticana): Typis Polyglottis Vaticanis, 1923-1939; Vols. VII-IX, ed. cura et studio Emī Iustiniani Card Seredi.), m.4622 (hereafter cited as *Fontes*).

36 Zitelli, *De Dispensationibus Matrimonialibus,* p. 175.

sanations of marriages in the early nineteenth century by Pope Pius VIII (1800-1823). The sanations were issued during the reign of Napoleon Bonaparte (1799-1814) for the validating of the many invalidly contracted marriages that occurred in the tumultuous and blood-drenched days of the French Revolution. Pope Pius granted the first of the two sanations on August 14, 1801, and the second on February 8, 1809.[37]

It was also during the Napoleonic regime that Cardinal Caprara received a delegation from the Holy See allowing him to give to the bishops of France the faculty of granting a *sanatio in radice.* Cardinal Caprara's instruction was dated April 25, 1803.[38]

Shortly after the middle of the nineteenth century Pope Pius IX (1846-1878) granted a general *sanatio in radice* to Austria. This dispensation was given on March 7, 1856.[39] Pope Leo XIII (1878-1903) granted a *sanatio in radice* on June 2, 1892.[40]

The beginning of the present century saw the issuance of Pope Pius X's (1903-1914) important apostolic letter *Provida* on January 18, 1906.[41] This document, which applied to the German Empire, sanated the marriages clandestinely entered into prior to April 15, 1906 by Catholics with non-Catholics. Pius X extended this concession to Hungary through a decree of the Sacred Congregation of the Sacraments on February 27, 1909, and in this instance the favor was granted to Orientals as well as to Latins.[42]

Article V.

The "Renewal of Consent" and *"ex nunc"-"ex tunc" Controversies*

Thomas Sanchez (1550-1610), an outstanding post-Tridentine canonical authority on matrimony, headed the group which held that a renewal of consent was necessary for the use of a *sanatio in radice.*

---

37 Wernz, Ius Decretalium, IV, n. 654, note 18: Cappello, *De Sacramentis,* V, *De Matrimonio,* n. 858, note 5.

38 Zitelli, *De Dispensationibus Matrimonialibus,* p. 175.

39 Cappello, *De Sacramentis,* V, *De Matrimonio,* n. 858, note 5.

40 *Loc. cit.*

41 *Fontes,* n. 670.

42 *Actae Apostolicae Sedis* (Romae, 1909-), I (1909), 516, 517 (hereafter cited as *AAS*).

Sanchez denied that the Pope had it within his power to dispense with the renewal of matrimonial consent, and he (Sanchez) added that without the renewal of consent the marriage would not be valid and therefore would not produce any legal effects.[43]

Apparently the view of Sanchez carried considerable weight, for in the succeeding one hundred and fifty years three authors adopted the opinion of Sanchez practically point for point.

The first of these authors was Gonzalez Tellez, who wrote in the second half of the seventeenth century. A text from the *Commentaria Perpetua* of Gonzalez Tellez shows the close adherence of his reasoning to that of Sanchez. The text is as follows: "Quoniam non dicimus (ut pro contraria opinione ponderat) Pontificem posse efficere, quod matrimonium fuerit a principio validum, vel quod nunc incipiat valere abvque novo contrihentium consensu, haec enim omnia planum est non subesse pontificiae potestati.[44]

The views of Corradus Pyrrhus (+ 1686) and of Pirhing (+ 1689), the other two of this group, are almost identical with that of Gonzalez Tellez.[45] Both of these authors, just as Gonzalez Tellez and as Sanchez before them, held that a marriage could not be validated by means of a *sanatio in radice* unless a renewal of consent was had, for the pope would be taking upon itself that which does not lie within his pontifical power.[46]

---

[43] Thomas Sanchez, *De Sancto Matrimonii Sacramento Disputationum Libri Tres,* (3 vols. Lugduni, 1669), Lib. VIII, disp. VII, n. 4: "Non enim dicimus posse nunc Pontificem efficere ut id matrimonium fuerit a principio firmum vel nunc incipiat valere absque novo contrahentium consensu, vel ut ex eo non sint secuti effectus iure civili statuti. Haec enim omnia aperte non subsunt pontificiae potestati."

[44] *Commentaria Perpetua in Singulos Textus Quinque Librorum Detretalium Gregorii IX* (5 vols., Lugduni, 1673), Lib. IV, tit. XVII, c. XIII, n. 22, *versus finem* (hereafter cited *Commentaria Perpetua*).

[45] Corradus Pyrrhus, *Praxis Dispensationum Apostolicarum* (Neapoli, 1641), Lib. VIII, c. III, n. 58: Pirhing, *Ius Canonicum in V Libros Decretalium* (5 vols. in 4, Dilingae, 1674-1678), Lib. IV, tit. XVII, c. VI, n. 42.

[46] Sanchez, *De Sancto Matrimonii Sacramento Disputationum Libri Tres,* Lib. VIII, disp. VII, n. 4: Gonzalez Tellez, *Commentaria Perpetua,* Lib. IV, tit, XVII, c. XIII, n. 22, *versus finem:* Corradus Pyrrhus, *Praxis Dispensationum Apostolicarum,* Lib. VIII, c. III, n. 58: Pirhing, *Ius Canonicum in V Libros Decretalium, loc. cit.*

Généstal (1872-1931) in his revision of Esmein's work observed that this view was initially taken by Sanchez.[47] And he seems to be corroborated by Perrone, who in his work on matrimony pointed out the dependency of Pirhing upon Sanchez.[48]

Before one may absolutely place Corradus Pyrrhus among those who staunchly defended the view requiring the renewal of consent, one must take cognizance of another text of his that seemingly contradicts the text cited above by the writer. In this latter text Corradus Pyrrhus stated that the petitioners to whom a *sanatio in radice* has been granted can remain in their original marriage contract, thereby implying that no new exchange of consent is needed.[49]

Despite the fact that Corradus Pyrrhus is usually listed with Sanchez, Gonzalez Tellez, and Pirhing as being one of the early authors who demanded a renewal of consent before the *sanatio in radice* could take effect, the discrepancy in his texts tends to indicate that his position in this matter is not as clear.

Anacletus Reiffenstuel (†1703) apparently did not delve into the problem of whether or not consent needed to be renewed by the parties in having their marriage validated by means of a *sanatio in radice.* He did discuss, however, other aspects of this manner of revalidation. This omission is, indeed, unfortunate, since Rieffenstuel's reasoning concerning other matters allied to this subject[50] gives promise that he would have undoubtedly influenced later canonists in their treatment of this problem.

Van Espen (1646-1728), although his span of life touched both the seventeenth and eighteenth centuries, is considered as an eighteenth century author. He wrote on marriage, but he did not give any particular attention to the *sanatio in radice.* Van Espen did hold, however, that all marriage validations required a new exchange of consent by the

[47] Esmein-Généstal, *Le Mariage en Droit Canonique,* (2 vols. Parisiis, 1929-1935, vol. I of Esmeins work published by R. Généstral in 1929, vol. II by Généstral and J. Dauvillier in 1935), II, p. 403.

[48] *De Matrimonio Christiano,* II, p. 162, note 29.

[49] Corradus Pyrrhus, *Op. cit.,* Lib. VIII, c. III, n. 50.

[50] Cf., *Ius Canonicum Universum,* Lib. IV, tit. XVII, nn. 48-51; V, Append. XIII. (5 vols. in 7, Parisiis, 1864-1870.)

parties involved.[51] This general statement by Van Espen would then seem to indicate that he includes the dispensation *sanatio in radice* as well as the other more frequently used forms of marriage validation.

Schmalzgrueber (†1735), a contemporary of Van Espen, was of the opinion that the mind of the Church in this problem was to have the parties renew their consent when a *sanatio in radice* was granted: but he also held that the opposing view was probable.[52] La Croix (†1714), the Jesuit moralist, also demanded a new exchange of consent.[53]

The author of the *Dictionaire de Droit Canonique*, Durand de Maillane (†1814), taught a renewal of consent to be required in a *sanatio in radice* if the consent had been wanting in the initial entrance of the parties into their marriage union.[54] Needless to say, this seems an evading of the question, and Durand proffered very little explanation, since the lack of consent in the original union obviously meant that no matrimonial intent ever existed. Whether or not Durand held as necessary a renewal of consent by the parties if their original consent persevered is not clear from his work.

The view of Sanchez, calling for a new exchange of consent by the parties in the event that a *sanatio in radice* was to be granted, seems to have lost its influence on the thinking of other canonists after the year 1775, for after that date the view was not prevalent at all. Sanchez and other canonists who adopted his view regarding the renewal of consent apparently gave no express consideration to the point of time in the marriage at which the validation takes effect. It would appear that since these authors held for the retroactivity of effects they likewise held that the validation took effect retroactively. This theory seems substantiated by the fact that Barbosa, who wrote in the same

---

[51] Cf.,*Opera Omnia Canonica In Sex Partes distributa, Pars prima-tertia complectens Iuris Ecclesiastici Universi, Hodiernae Disciplinae praesertim Belgii, Galliae, Germaniae, & vincinarum Provinciarum accomodati, Primam Partem: cum additionibus, quae in supplemento extabant, suis locis diligenter insertis* (6 vols. in 3, Lovanii, 1732), I, pars II, tit, XIV, c. 5. nn. 9, 11.

[52] Cf., *Ius Ecclesiasticum Universum* (5 vols in 12, Romae, 1843-1845), Lib. IV, tit. XVI, n. 268.

[53] Cf., *Theologia Moralis,* II, Lib. VI, pars III, dub 3, nn. 809-812.

[54] Cf., *Dictionnaire de Droit Canonique* (3. ed., 4 vols., Lyons, 1770), s.v. *legitimation, mariage, rehabilitation.*

century as Gonzalez Tellez, explicitly mentions the validation of the marriage as taking effect retroactively.

In the following pages the writer will trace the opposing view, which did not demand a new exchange of consent, but which at the same time reflected a division on the question as to the time when the validation became effective.

Before examining the opinion that stands contrary to the view presented above, the writer deems it advisable to place the group that held that no new exchange of consent was necessary in a *sanatio in radice* into two distinct divisions. All of the canonists teaching this view were in accord in regard to the following: when a *sanatio in radice* was granted, no new exchange of consent by the parties is required, because the original consent persevered and therefore sufficed. They disagreed, however, in respect to the exact point of time in the marriage when the validation took effect.

One division of this group claimed that the validation took effect retroactively, or *ex tunc,* and so the validation was effected *in radice* in every sense of the phrase. As a result the marriage was validated from the very moment of its initial inception. The other division maintained that the validation took effect only from the time that the dispensation was granted, although the juridical and canonical effects of the *sanatio in radice* were operative retroactively in the original exchange of consent.

Barbosa (†1649), a noted post-Tridentine author, left no doubt as to the view he advocated. In referring to the power of the Roman pontiff to effect a marriage validation he explicity used the words *ex tunc* as showing his definite preference for a retroactive validating effect.[55]

Barbosa later on in this same work wrote that no fiction of law was involved in the dispensation, but that by virtue of the declared *sanatio in radice* the marriage always has been valid.[56]

Rigantius (†1735), the author who first recorded Pope Boniface's VIII's granting of what is believed to have been the first dispensation

---

[55] A. Barbosa, *Vorotum Decisivorum, et Consultativorum Canonicorum Libri II,* (2 vols. in 1, Lugduni, 1663-1664), Lib. II, votum XXVII, n. 1. (hereafter cited as *Vota*): ". . . efficere ut ex tunc verum matrimonium remaneat, ac si illud ab initiovalidum intervenisset."

[56] *Op. cit.,* Lib. II, votum XXVII, n. 15.

in radice matrimonii, was very clear in stating that when the Pope dis pensed *in radice* no new exchange of consent by the parties was required.[57]

However, although Regantius used the words *ex tunc* in speaking of the dispensation *in radice,* he was rather ambiguous. It is not plain whether Rigantius was speaking of the validation of the marriage or the juridical effects thereof, when he sued the words *ex tunc.*[58]

Despite the ambiguity of Rigantius' text, this author may be counted with the group holding that the validation of the marriage was effected retroactively. Scherer (1845-1918) also vigorously proposed this view.[59]

Other leading writers of the mid-nineteenth century were convinced that by a *sanatio in radice* a validation of a marriage was effected from its very beginning. Perrone, whose view on another historical point of the *sanatio in radice* has been cited elsewhere in this study, was one of these writers.[60]

Giovine, whose view concerning the date for the granting of the first *sanatio in radice* coincided with that of Perrone, also followed Perrone in the controversy concerning the point of time in the marriage when a validation resulting from a *sanatio in radice* took effect.[61]

Brillaud, writing shortly after Perrone and Giovine, holds the same view as do these latter two authors.[62]

Théphany, another contemporary of Perrone and Giovine, followed their line of thought and arrived at the same conclusion.[63]

The theory which proposed that a retroactive validation was effected through a *sanatio in radice* was extant at the close of the nineteenth century. Apparently the authors who proposed this view never quesioned the tenability of the argument in behalf of their position. Yet later authors were very quick to note the metaphysical impossibility of

---

[57] *Commentaria in Regueas,* Tom. IV, Reg. L, n. 106.

[58] *Ibid.,* n. 107.

[59] Cf., *Handbuch des Kirchenrechtes,* (2 vols., Graz, 1898), II, 507-510.

[60] Cf., *De Matrimonio Christiano,* II, pp. 147-152.

[61] Cf., *De Dispensationibus Matrimonialibus,* I, consult. XXIII, sect. 23.

[62] Cf., *Traité Pratique des Dispenses de Mariage,* pp. 57, 279, apud Wernz-Vidal, *Ius Matrimoniale,* p. 877, note 41. The work of Brillaud is not available to the writer.

[63] Cf., *Traité des Dispenses Matrimoniales* (Paris, 1889), pp. 232, 236.

changing, in reality, what had been one thing (invalidity) into its direct opposite (validity) merely through the issuing of a dispensation.[64] With the advent of the twentieth century and the promulgation of the Code of Canon Law this view became obsolete. The Code in 1918 changed into fact what a few years earlier Cardinal Gasparri in his pre-Code tract had prophesied in theory.[65]

Gutierrez (†c. 1625) appears to have been the first author to proffer the view which abstracted from any need of the renewal of consent by the parties when they received a *sanatio in radice.* In proposing his theory, Gutierrez also seemed to be the first to hold that the validation when effected through a *sanatio in radice* took effect only at the time the dispensation was granted, and was not retroactive. Gutierrez did, however, admit the retroactivity of the canonical effects.[66]

Many authors in the succeeding one hundred and fifty years followed Gutierrez in denying that a new exchange of consent was required in connection with the granting of a *sanatio in radice.* But few, with the possible exception of Pope Benedict XIV and St. Alphonsus Liguori (†1787), agreed with him in saying that the validation took effect as of the time when the dispensation was granted. In the nineteenth century, however, many authors entered the controversy and sided with this view. Carrière (1775-1864) accepted the theory of Gutierrez. Other noteworthy authors, likewise, aligned themselves with Gutierrez in rejecting the need for a renewal of consent and also in restricting the validation as being effective in time only simultaneously with the granting of the dispensation. Martin (†1859), Gury (†1866), and Feije (†1894) may be listed in this group.[67]

---

[64] A. Vermeersch-J. Creusen, *Epitome Iuris Canonici,* (3 vols., Vol. II, 6. ed., Brugis, 1940), II, n. 455: Gasparri, *Tractatus Canonicus de Matrimonio* (2 vols., Nova ed., ad mentem Codicis, *Romae: Typis Polyglottis Vaticanis,* 1932), II, n. 1208: Wernz-Vidal, *Ius Matrimoniale,* n. 670, note 41.

[65] Cf. *Tractatus Canonicus de Matrimonio* (3. ed., 2 vols., Parisiis, 1904), II, pp. 313, 315, n. 1149.

[66] Cf., *Canonicae Quaestiones* (3 vols .in 2, Lugduni, 1661), III, c. 23, nn. 4, 23, 32.

[67] Carrière, *De Matrimonio,* (2. ed., 2 vols., Parisiis, Apud Mequignon Juniorem, 1842, joined to *De Justitia,* 1854), II, 547; Martin, *De Matrimonio et potestate ipsum dirimendi, ecclesiae soli exclusive propria* (2 vols., Lugduni, Parisiis, Apud Perisse Fratres, 1844) p. 438; Gury, *Compendium Theologiae*

Sagmüller (†1942) and Cardinal Gasparri (†1934), who wrote in the early twentieth century, a relatively short time before the *Codex Iuris Canonici* was promulgated, were the last important pre-Code authors to treat of this problem. They taught that no renewal of consent was needed in a *sanatio in radice* and that the validation was not retroactive.[68] Needless to say, the influence that Cardinal Gasparri had upon the codification is readily seen in the canons dealing with the *sanatio in radice.*[69] In these canons Gasparri's opinions formulate the gist of the law.

We have seen the various trends of thought as to whether or not the parties are to be required to renew their matrimonial consent upon receiving a *sanatio in radice* dispensation from the Church and the opinions concerning the time when this dispensation takes effect. It is to be noted that the view requiring a new exchange of consent passed into oblivion about the year 1775. This was true despite the fact that many celebrated canonists had adopted the view previously. In retrospect it is also interesting to note that even after the contrary view which rejected the requirement of a renewal of consent had become practically unanimous among commentators the members of the group holding this doctrine disagreed among themselves on whether the dispensation validated the marriage at the point of time when the consent was initially exchanged or at the point of time when the dispensation was granted. With the promulgation of the *Codex Iuris Canonici* in 1918 all controversies concerning the above mentioned points were suppressed. The Code definitely eliminated the speculative possibility that a new exchange of consent is required from the parties involved. It explicity stated that, while the canonical effects are, as a rule, made effective by a fiction of law retroactively to the time of the original matrimonial consent itself, the validation is obtained only from the moment when the dispensation is granted.[70]

Moralis (Edit. Romana, Ex Typographia Polyglotta S.C. de Prop. Fide, Romae, 1872), p. 877, n. 907: Feije, *De Impedimentis et Dispensationibus Matrimonialibus,* p. 772.

[68] Gasparri, *Tractatus Canonicus de Matrimonio,* (2 vols. 3. ed., Parisiis, 1904), II, pp. 314, 315, n. 1149: Sägmüller, *Lehrbuch des Katholischen Kirchenrechts,* (3 vols., Breisgau, 1904), II, p. 218, n. 11.

[69] Canons 1138-1141.

[70] Canon 1138, §§1-2.

Article VI. Benedict XIV and the *Sanatio in Radice*

Pope Benedict XIV concerned himself more than did any other Pontiff with the *sanatio in radice.* However, it would not be correct to restrict Benedict XIV's interest in this type of matrimonial dispensation to the eighteen years (1740-1758) during which he held the highest office of the Roman Catholic Church. At least twenty years before he ascended the Chair of Peter, Benedict had shown a keen interest in this extraordinary type of dispensation. As the ensuing years passed, Benedict's interest increased and apparently his views on different phases of the *sanatio in radice* changed.

In the year 1720, Benedict (then Prosper Lambertini) took a stand in the controversy, then in full sway, concerning the necessity for a renewal of consent in conjunction with a sanation. Apparently using a decision of the Sacred Roman Rota as his guide, he accepted the view eliminating a renewal of consent.[71] Although Benedict reiterated this view the same year[73] citing Barbosa as a support to his view, he seemingly wavered in 1726, as in that year he inclined toward the view calling for a new exchange of consent.[74] By the year 1731 Benedict had reverted to his original line of thinking. Once more he adopted the view that a new exchange of consent by the parties receiving the *sanatio in radice* was not necessary. As a basis for his return to this opinion, Benedict cited Pope Clement XI, although Clement's grant of a *sanatio in radice* had been made some thirty years earlier, when he issued his Constitution *Apostolicae dignitatis* in 1701.[75] Why Benedict did not advert to Clement's grant in formulating his views in 1720 and 1726 is not known.

Eight years after Benedict has assumed the duties of the papacy, he wrote his work *De Synodo Dioecesana,* in which he upheld his original

---

[71] Cf., *Opera Omnia* (Novissima Edit., Venetis, 1788, 15 vols. in 7), XIV, *Quaestiones Canonicae,* q. 183, n. 25, sqq. (Hereafter referred to as *Quaestiones-Canonicae.*)

[73] *Quaestiones Canonicae,* q. 174.

[74] *Op. cit.,* q. 527.

[75] Cf., *Opera Omnia, Institutiones Ecclesiasticae,* Lib. XI, p. 87, n. 80. (Hereafter cited as *Institutiones Ecclesiasticae*).

view, citing as authorities two of his predecessors, Clement XI (1700-1721) and Clement XII (1730-1740.)[76]

The three works of Benedict here cited were private writings of the canonist pope, and therefore none of the opinions expressed in these works may be attributed to Benedict as reflecting the official view of Rome. Only one official document of Benedict XIV touched the controversy concerning the renewal of consent. This document, the Constitution *Esti matrimonialis,* restated his doctrine that no renewal of consent was required as a condition for the granting of a *sanatio in radice.*[77]

Pope Benedict XIV was highly respected by later canonists, commentators, and authors, and his arguments greatly influenced the opinions formulated by those who followed him. Once Benedict had definitely taken the stand that no new exchange of consent was necessary in a *sanatio in radice,* later authors unequivocally adopted his argumentation. Benedict's reign as Pope came to a close in 1758, and by the year 1775 the doctrine calling for a renewal of consent in a *sanatio in radice* could be regarded as a canonical relic.

However clear Benedict may have been in expressing his opinion that no new exchange of consent by the parties was necessary in order that they might reecive the benefit of such a matrimonial dispensation, he seemed to be just as obscure in his view on whether the validation of the marriage took effect retroactively or was effective only from the time when the dispensation was granted. Authors since the time of Benedict have been in constant disagreement as to just what exactly was Benedict's thought on the matter. Wernz (1842-1914) and Vidal (1867-1938), saw in Benedict a weighty authority for the doctrine that denied retroactivity to the validation. Cardinal Gasparri also understood Benedict as endorsing this view.[78]

Among those who saw in Benedict a strong advocate of the theory claiming that the validation of the marriage was effective retroactively

---

[76] Cf., *Opera Omnia, De Synodo Dioecesana,* Lib. XIII, cap. VII, n. XXI (hereafter cited *De Synodo Dioecesana*).

[77] *Bullarii Romani Continuatio Summorum Pontificum* (19 vols., Prati, 1756-1883), III, pars II, pp. 288-291.

[78] Wernz-Vidal, *Ius Matrimoniale,* n. 558, note 12: Gasparri, *Tractatus Canonicus de Matrimonio,* II, n. 1209.

to the initial exchange of consent were Perrone, Scherer, Thephany, and Brillaud.[79]

Those who held that Benedict favored the "ex tunc" theory based their claim on Benedict's *De Synodo Dicesana* in which he definitely taught that the legetimation of children retroactive to the first exchange of consent was an effect of the *sanatio in radice.* In the same context he spoke of the validation of the marriage. According to those who maintained that its effects occurred "ex tunc," he implied that the validation itself was retroactive to the initial exchanging of consent.[80] The group which proposed this view also had recourse to the *Quaestiones Canonicae* of Benedict XIV.[81]

Those who contended for the opposite or "ex nunc" opinion cited the same work but, abstracting from *Quaestio* 527, they appealed to *Quaestio* 174. The text, taken from the *De Synodo Diocesana,* is an indication of how each group took Benedict's works and construed the interpretation so as to conclude that Benedict undoubtedly held its point of view. Using the same text, the various authors arrived at directly contradictory conclusions. Thèphany cited the text in behalf of the *"ex tunc"* argument,[82] whereas Gury, Wernz and Vidal used the identical text in support of the *"ex nunc"* view.[83]

Besides the bearing that Benedict XIV's works had on the question of the renewal of consent and on the *"ex tunc"-"ex nunc"* phases of the *sanatio in radice,* his works advert also to other aspects of the dispensation. Benedict refuted for instance one of the early objections raised against the *sanatio in radice.* This objection was based on an alleged text of Pope Gregory XIII, in which Gregory repeatedly denied that the Pope had the power to grant a *sanatio in radice.* Benedict staunchly defended the power of the papacy, and said that, if Gregory ever did make such a statement, he was speaking of only one particular case in which for certain reasons the Pope was unable to grant this dispensa-

[79] Perrone, *De Matrimonio Christiano,* II, 147-152: Scherer *Handbuch des Kirchenrechts,* II, p. 510, note 42: Thephany, *Traité des Dispenses Matrimoniales,* pp. 232-236: Brillaud, *Traité Pratique des Dispenses de Mariage,* pp. 57, 279.

[80] *De Synodo Diocesana,* Lib. XIII, cap. 21, 7.

[81] *Quaestiones Canonicae,* q. 527.

[82] *Traité des Dispenses Matrimoniales,* p. 231.

[83] Gury, *Compendium Theologiae Moralis,* p. 877, n. 901: Wernz-Vidal, *Ius Matrimoniale,* p. 859, note 12.

tion. Pichler (1670-1736) upheld the argument of Benedict, and the refutation by Benedict came to be commonly accepted by the authors.[84]

The influence which the writings of Benedict had upon later canonists cannot be overestimated: the wealth of information concerning the *sanatio in radice* that Benedict possessed is still reflected in the views of present day commentators upon this dispensation.

Article VII. The Origin of the Fiction of Law

The manner in which the effects of a *sanatio in radice* are produced retroactively to the point at which the initial exchange of consent took place is called a fiction of law. The Code states this fact explicity in canon 1138.[85] Although the canonists appear to be the first to explain the retroactivity of juridical effect by a fiction of law,[86] this explanation for retroactivity is not at all novel with them, since for its origin one may look to Roman Law.[87]

In Roman Law the fiction of law is found in the Digest and in the Institutes of Justinian.[88] The chief purpose of the inserting of the fiction of law into the *Corpus Iuris Civilis* was to protect the rights of a Roman soldier dying in captivity. The fiction worked in such a way that when the soldier died in the hands of the enemy he was construed *per fictionem iuris* as having expired on Roman soil and so received the juridical posthumous rights that would have been his had he in fact passed away in Rome.[89] The application of this fiction of law in the *Corpus Iuris Civilis* is called the *Lex Cornelia.*[90]

84 Benedictus XIV, *Quaestiones Canonicae,* q. 174; Pichler, *Ius Canonicum Secundum Quinque Decretalium Titulos Gregorii IX,* (2 vols., Venetiis, 1741), I, Lib. IV, tit. 17, n. 18: Harrigan, p. 31: Wernz-Vidal, *Ius Matrimonials,* p. 864, note 20.

85 Canon 1138, §1. Matrimonii in radice sanatio est eiusdem convalidatio, . . . per fictionem iuris, circa effectus canonicus, ad praeteritum.

86 Carriere, *De Matrimonio,* II, 548: Palmieri, *Tractatus de Matrimonio Christiano* (Romae, 1880), p. 300: Gasparri, *De Matrimonio,* II, n. 1209: Cappello, *De Sacramentis,* V, *De Matrimonio* n. 851: Wernz-Vidal, *Ius Matrimoniale,* n. 661.

87 Jean Bernhard, "*L'Explication Juridique de la Retroactivite de la Sanatio in Radice Dans la Doctrine Canonique Moderne,*" *Ephemerides Iuris Canonici* (Romae 1945-), VII (1951), 80-88.

88 Insti. 2(12.5), D. 28(1.12), 49(15.18)

89 Inst. *loc. cit.;* D. *loc. cit.*

90 *Loc. cit.*

The application of the *Lex Cornelia* to the Roman soldier dying in captivity exemplifies the standard definition of fiction of law by Alciatus (1492-1550). This author defined a fiction of law as "a rule of law which assumes as true for a just cause, something which is false but not impossible."[91]

Thus in a fiction of law, as seen from the *Corpus Iuris Civilis* and Alciatus' definition, the effects that become retroactive must be possible, although in reality they are false. This same principle was adopted by the canonists who applied it to the *sanatio in radice,* thus legally explaining how the validation of a marriage could also contain retroactive effects.

The disagreement among the authors concerning the *sanatio in radice* was not restricted to the problems concerning the legitimation of offspring, the dispensation from the renewal of consent, and the point of time in the continuance of marital union at which the validation of the marriage took effect, it also touched the manner in which these effects flowed from this dispensation.

Although the authors did disagree on the last mentioned point, the promulgation of the *Codex Iuris Canonici* in 1918 settled the dispute. For in canon 1138, § 1 the Code explicity states that this production of the effects of the sanation retroactively to the past is done by a fiction of law (*per fictionem iuris*). Apparently the basis for the *fictio iuris* in the Code is the *Lex Cornelia* of Roman Law.[92]

Sanchez in his view obviated the need for explaining the retroactivity of the effects through a legal manner, for in his text he simply took it for granted that the papal power produced the required legal effects.[93] Gonzalez Tellez, Pirhing, and Corradus Pyrrhus accepted the view of Sanchez.[94]

Barbosa was in accord with the above-mentioned view although, as

---

[91] Thus quoted in Cicognani, *Canon Law,* (2. ed., Philadelphia, Dulphin Press, 1935), pp. 535-536.

[92] Cf., *Inst.* 2(12.5), D. 28(1.12), D. 49(15.18).

[93] *De Sancto Matrimonii Sacramento,* Lib. VIII, disp. 7, n. 4.

[94] Gonzalez Tellez, *Commentaria Perpetua,* Lib. IV, tit. XVII, cap. XIII, n. 23: Pirhing, *Ius Canonicum,* Lib. IV. tit. 17, n. 26: Corradus Pyrrhus, *Praxis Dispensationum Apostolicarum,* Lib. VIII, c. 5. n. 58.

was noted previously, he differed from Sanchez on the *"ex tunc-ex nunc"* question.[95]

Rigantius did not use the expression *fictio iuris.* However, his explanation of how the Pope was able to sanate an invalid marriage by applying the effects retroactively to the beginning of the union, may be identified with what is meant by a fiction of law.[96]

Pope Benedict XIV likewise did not use the expression *fictio iuris,* but his explanation leaves little doubt as to his acceptance of the fiction of law explanation.[97]

Many authors seem to have abstracted from the manner in which the effects of the validated marriage were produced retroactively, and they omitted all mention of any fiction of law.[98]

Feije, however, claimed that the retroactive production of the effects by a *sanatio in radice* was effected through a fiction of law.[99]

Perrone, on the other hand, reverted to the view of Barbosa.[100] Carrière accepted the fiction of law theory, but in addition he claimed that the effects of a sanation were of two distinct kinds, real effects and true effects.[101] In developing Carrière's view Gury limited the effects to only the real effects, which view seems contradictory to the Roman Law doctrine.[102] Cardinal Gasparri in the nineteenth century wrote what appears to be the explanation *par excellance* of the fiction of law theory as it then obtained.[103]

---

95 *Vota,* Lib. II, votum XXVII, n. 29.

96 *Commentaria in Regulas,* Reg. L, nn. 106, 118.

97 *Quaestiones Canonicae,* qq. 183, 527.

98 Schmalzgrueber, *Ius Ecclesiasticum Universum,* L.o. IV, tit. 17, n. 123: Théphany, *Traité des Dispenses Matrimoniales,* p. 230: Sägmüller, *Lehrbuch des Katholischen Kirchenrechts,* II, 218, 219: Rosset, *De Sacramento Matrimonii Tractatus Dogmaticus, Muralis, Liturgicus et Iudiciarius* (6 vols., Parisiis, 1895-1896), IV, 260.

99 *De Impedimentis et Dispensationibus Matrimonialibus,* p. 772.

100 *De Matrimonio Christiano,* II, p. 159, note 22.

101 *De Matrimonio,* II, 548.

102 *Compendium Theologiae Moralis,* II, p. 877.

103 *Tractatus Canonicus de Matrimonio,* (2 vols., Parisiis, 1891-1892), II, p. 315, n. 1149.

PART II

CANONICAL COMMENTARY

CHAPTER I

General Notions of the "Sanatio in Radice"

Article I: The *Sanatio* as a Dispensation

A *sanatio in radice* or radical sanation is the convalidation of a marriage. It involves, besides the dispensation or cessation of the impediment, a dispensation from the law of the renewing of consent, and a retroaction, through a fiction of the law, concerning the canonical effects, to the past.[1] Hence a radical sanation is a matrimonial dispensation employed by the Church for the convalidating of a marriage that previously was contracted invalidly owing to the presence of a diriment impediment or because of defect of form. Generally a sanation is categorized as a dispensation, and so the first step in juridically analyzing a *sanatio* is to determine what kind of dispensation it is.

According to canon 80 a dispensation is a relaxation of the law in a special case. Vermeersch-Creusen define a matrimonial dispensation as a "legitimate act of a superior by which the obligation of a law prohibiting marriage, with or without the nullity of the contract, is relaxed in a special case."[2] O'Keeffe in his work on matrimonial dispensations[3] gives the detailed definition of De Smet:[4] "an act of a legitimate power by which in a particular case, or in regard to a particular person, the law is relaxed in its force invalidating or prohibiting matrimony, that force of the law remaining in respect to other members of the community and in respect to other cases."

Matrimonial dispensations may be further subdivided into dispensations *ante factum* and dispensations *post factum* or *adcontrahendum*

[1] Canon 1138 §1.

[2] *Epitome Iuris Canonici*, II, n. 301.

[3] *Matrimonial Dispensations, Powers of Bishops, Priests, and Confessors*, The Catholic University of America Canon Law Studies, n. 45, (Washington, D.C.: The Catholic University of America, 1927), p. 3.

[4] *De Sponsalibus et Matrimonio* (2 vols., ed. 3, Brugis: Car. Beyaert, 1920, 1923.) I, n. 382: "actus potestatis legitimae quo in casu particulari, aut quoad personan particularem, relaxatur lex in sua vi irritante vel prohibente matrimonium, manente illa vi legis quoad reliqua membra communitatis aut alios casus." (ed. 4, 1927 uses the same wording in n. 782.)

and *ad convalidandum.*[5] A radical sanation is obviously to be classified in the *post factum* or *ad convalidadum* type of dispensation, since its primary purpose is to convalidate a marriage. The dispensation is granted not before but after the attempted marriage. A *sanatio in radice* may be termed a pontifical dispensation in contradistinction to an episcopal or non-pontifical dispensation.[6] The Apostolic See or one delegated by the Apostolic See is able to grant a *sanatio in radice.*[7] This classification is made even though local ordinaries in their faculties are empowered to grant certain sanations. They do so as delegates of the Holy See.

As a rule matrimonial dispensations also are distinguished in accordance with the manner of their granting, namely in the external forum or in the internal forum.[8] No clear cut distinction of this nature, however, may be made in regard to a *sanatio in radice,* for sanations are granted in both the internal and the external forum. The Holy See utilizes various Sacred Congregations in the granting of sanations, and gives to these Congregations, with the orbit of the power that the individual Congregation possesses, the competency to grant sanations. For example, The Holy Office is competent to grant sanations for marriages that are invalid because of the impediment of disparity of cult.[9] The Sacred Congregation of the Sacraments has competency for all sanations in the external forum save those that are definitely reserved to another Congregation e.g. marriages invalidated by the impediment of disparity of cult, or cases of mixed marriages generally.[10] According to Harrigan the Congregation for the Propagation of the Faith has competency to grant sanations in mission countries[11] and the Sacred Congregation for

[5] Wernz-Vidal, *Ius Matromoniale,* p. 517, n. 404.; Payen, *De Matrimonio in Missionalibus,* III, p. 607, n. 2743.; Cappello, *De Matrimonio,* p. 218, n. 220; Vermeersch-Creusen, *Epitome Iuris Canonici,* II, p. 212, n. 302.

[6] Cf. preceding footnote.

[7] Canon 1141.

[8] Wernz-Vidal, *Ius Matrimoniale,* p. 517, n. 404 I; Vermeersch-Cheusen, *Epitome Iuris Canonici,* III, p. 212, n. 302; Cappello, *De Sacramentis, V, De Matrimonio,* p. 216, n. 220; Payen, *De Matriomino in Missionibus,* III, p. 607, n. 2743.

[9] Canon 247; Harrigan, pp. 120, 121.

[10] Canon 249; Harrigan, pp. 121-123; Cappello, *De Sacramentis,* V, *De Matrimonio,* n. 855.

[11] *The Radical Sanation of Invalid Marriages,* pp. 123-125.

the Oriental Church has competency to grant *sanationes in radice* for all marriages affecting Orientals, save those that are reserved to the Holy Office.[12] Whenever the above-mentioned Congregations grant sanations they do so in the external forum. The Sacred Penitentiary alone grants sanations in the internal forum, which grant it can make in either the sacramental or the non-sacramental internal forum.[13] A *sanatio in radice* therefore will be a dispensation granted in the internal or external forum according to whether it is granted by the Sacred Penitentiary or by one of the Sacred Congregations. Sanations granted by delegated persons, e.g. by local ordinaries, are granted in the external forum.

Upon this brief consideration of the various divisions of dispensations, it may be said that a *sanatio in radice* is a pontifical, *post factum* (or *ad convalidandum*) matrimonial dispensation that may be granted either in the internal or in the external forum.

Article II. Character of the Dispensation

As has been stated in the preceding article the *sanatio in radice* is a matrimonial dispensation or favor granted by the Church. However, to describe a sanation as merely a matrimonial dispensation would be a gross understatement, for a radical sanation is a very special kind of favor, an extraordinary type of favor whose extraordinary character is evidenced both by its nature and by its mode of operation.

A radical sanation is not simply *a* favor granted by the Apostolic See; rather, its essence is such that a *sanatio* is four distinct favors embodied in one grant by the Church. These four favors are explicitly enumerated in the Code[14] and are the following: (1) the convalidation of the previously invalid marriage; (2) the dispensation from the impediment that caused the marriage to be invalid, unless the impediment has ceased to exist; (3) the dispensation from the law requiring the renewal of consent by the parties involved, and lastly (4) the retroaction to the past, by means of a fiction of law, concerning the canonical

[12] Canon 257; Harrigan, pp. 126-130.

[13] Canons 258, §1; 1047; Harrigan, pp. 130-134.

[14] Canon 1138, §1.

effects.[15] These favors are not granted individually by the Church; they are contained in the single concession of a *sanatio* to the one petitioning it, since such is the nature of this extraordinary favor.

The four favors contained in a radical sanation do not unfold in a logical sequence in the order in which they receive mention in canon 1138, §1. In the logical order the first favor granted should be the dispensation from the impediment causing the invalidity of the marriage, unless this hindrance has ceased to exist. The placing of this favor first is absolutely necessary, since no marriage can be convalidated or the effects of the convalidation produced until the legal obstacle preventing the validity of the contract has been removed. The second favor granted, in the logical order, should be the dispensation from the law requiring the renewal of consent by the parties whose marriage is being sanated. In the convalidating of a marriage, once the impediment causing the invalidity is removed, the next step is to have the parties renew their consent.[16]. The actual convalidation of the marriage itself should be the third favor to be considered in the logical order, for the convalidation is effected upon the removing of the diriment impediment and the neutralizing of the law which normally requires the renewing of consent.[17] The last favor granted in the logical order should be the retroaction, through a fiction of law, of the canonical effects to the past. Effects cannot be produced until their cause, in this instance the convalidating of the marriage, occurs and so the retroactivity by a fiction of law and producing of the canonical effects logically follows the grant of the third favor, namely the convalidation of the marriage.

In the order of time there is no distinguishing features among the four favors contained in a *sanatic in radice.* Since all of the favors are embodied in the one grant of a radical sanation by the Church the favors naturally are conceded simultaneously.

Another extraordinary feature of the *sanatio in radice* is the power required to grant this favor. Canon 1141 reserves to the Apostolic See alone the right under common law to grant a radical sanation. The

---

[15] Bernhard, "Propos sur la Nature Juridique de la *'Sanatio in Radice'* dans le Droit Canonique Actuel,"—*Ephermerides Iuris Canonici,* IV (1948), p. 390.

[16] Canon 1133, §1.

[17] Canon 1133, §1.; O'Keeffe, p. 2.

question arises, however, as to whether or not the *Code of Canon Law* in making the benign concessions of faculties in canons 1043 and 1045 to ordinaries, includes in these grants the power to radically sanate a marriage as a means of convalidation. The writer does not intend to discuss on this question at length or to give an involved explanation as an answer but rather accepts the common view of canonists[18] who hold that the faculties accorded to local ordinaries for the convalidating of marriages according to the norms of canons 1043 and 1045 do not empower them to sanate marriages. The fact that the Holy See does not give the power to grant sanations in virtue of canons 1043 and 1045, but reserves that power to itself and to those to whom it expressly gives delegation furnished added evidence of the special character of the *sanatio in radice.*

Although the canonists cited above in connection with the consideration of canons 1043 and 1045 are quite explicit and definite in claiming that a *sanatio in radice* may not be granted in virtue of these canons, the same canonists, Cappello excepted, are silent regarding the question whether or not an ordinary is empowered by the Code to grant a sanation in virtue of canon 81. Since these writers, though they be silent concerning canon 81, reject the idea that a radical sanation may be granted in virtue of canons 1043 and 1045, and at the same time cite canon 1141[19] to support their argument, Harrigan[20] sees in their silence an implied rejection that a radical sanation may be granted through the powers conceded to ordinaries by canon 81.[21]

[18] Gasparri, *De Matrimonio,* I, p. 233, n. 396; Cappello, *De Matrimonio,* p. 229, n. 231; Wernz-Vidal, *Ius Matrimoniale,* p. 534, n. 413; Lydon, *Marriage Legislation in the New Code of Canon Law,* n. 72; Motry, *Diocesan Faculties According to the Code of Canon Law,* The Catholic University of America Canon Law Studies, n. 16 (Washington, D.C.; The Catholic University of America, 1922), p. 134; Harrigan, pp. 171-177; O'Keeffe, p. 92; Brennan, *Simple Convalidation of Marriage,* The Catholic University of America Canon Law Studies, n. 102 (Washington, D.C.; The Catholic University of America, 1937), p. 101.

[19] "Sanatio in radice concedi unice potest ab Apostolica Sede."

[20] *The Radical Sanation of Invalid Marriages,* p. 168.

[21] A generalibus ecclesiae legibus Ordinarii infra Romanum Pontificem dispensare nequeunt, ne in casu quidem peculiari, nisi haec potestas eisdem fuerit explicite vel implicite concessa, aut nisi difficilis sit recursus ad Sanctam Sedem

Bouuaert-Simenon explicitly deny that canon 81 contains the power to grant a *sanatio in radice*,[22] as did Payen (†1941).[23] who used canon 1040 as the basis for his view and argued from the general to the particular.

The writer does not agree with Harrigan in holding that the authors cited in reference to canons 1043 and 1045 by their silence imply that canon 81 does not empower local ordinaries to grant radical sanations. Since these authors explicity mention canons 1043 and 1045, the writer is of the opinion that they would have mentioned canon 81 had they desired to include that canon in their rejection. To the writer the silence of these authors indicates nothing other than that they are foregoing a positive consideration of the question. The writer, however, does accept Harrigan's view on the ultimate solution of the question, for he believes that the argument which Harrigan offers is of a compelling character.

Harrigan claims that although canon 81 is more inclusive than canons 1043 and 1045, since these latter two are concerned only with a matrimonial dispension that is to be given in a time of danger of death or when all things are prepared for a marriage, whereas canon 81 treats of any dispensation that the Holy See is wont to give, yet canon 81 does not accord the power to grant a radical sanation.

The gist of Harrigan's argument is that canon 81 enables an ordinary to dispense from ecclesiastical laws provided that the conditions of the canon are fulfilled. Since an impediment of the ecclesiastical law and the law requiring the renewal of consent by the parties are of ecclesiastical origin, it seems that an ordinary could grant a sanation by using canon 81 inasmuch as the dispensation from these two elements forms the nucleus of the convalidation to be effected by means of the radical sanation. However, retroaction of canonical effects to the past likewise is an essential part of a sanation, and it cannot be separated from the other dispensations embodied in the sanation. Ordinaries do not have the power to give retroactivity to canonical effects, since this

et simul in mora sit periculum gravis damni, et de dispensatione agatur quae a Sede Apostolica concedi solet.

22 Bouuaert-Simenon, *Manuale Juris Canonici* (3 vols., Vols. 1 and III, 5 ed.; Vol. II, 3 ed; Gandae et Leodii, 1 [1939], II [1947], III [1943]), *De Sacramentis,* n. 249, §2.

23 *De Matrimonio in Missionibus,* II, n. 2618.

power is not given them in the common law. Nor may it be argued that this power is given to ordinaries implicity. For it is not received in virtue of canon 66, §3, or of canon 200, §1, which canons are respectively concerned with the use of habitual faculties and delegated power. Retroaction in itself is not a mere dispensation, and so canon 81 cannot be regarded as making room for its application. Since the power to grant retroaction is not possessed by ordinaries, and since it is not accorded in canon 81, but is essential to the very concept of a *sanatio in radice,* one must simply conclude that ordinaries cannot grant a radical sanation in virtue of canon 81. This conclusion serves to emphasize all the more notably the extraordinary nature of the *sanatio in radice,* and accords fully with the manifest impart of canon 1141.

Article III. Method in Which the Favor is Granted

The *sanatio in radice* is a favor granted by ecclesiastical authority: this fact is established in canon 1138. Being a favor the radical sanation is granted by way of a rescript[24] and the time at which the favor becomes effective depends upon the manner in which the favor is granted in the rescript.[25] There are two methods in which the Church is accustomed to grant favors: the first method is by granting them *in forma commissoria* and the second method is by granting them *in forma gratiosa.*[26]

In the grant of a favor *in forma commissoria* the favor is granted through the medium of an executor. Therefore the favor is not conceded directly by the grantor to the petitioner, but rather the grantor deputes an intermediary who carries out the grant. In a favor of this nature the favor does not take effect until the time of its execution by

[24] Canon 36.

[25] Canon 38.

[26] Canon 38: Cappello, *Summa Iuris Canonici,* (3 vols., Vol. I, 5th ed., Romae, 1951.), I, nn. 133 §3, 140; Beste, *Introductio in Codicem* (3 ed., Collegeville, Minn., St. John's Abbey Press, 1946), p. 110; O'Neill, *Papal Rescripts of Favor* The Catholic University of America Canon Law Studies, n. 57 (Washington, D.C., The Catholic University of America, 1930.), p. 156. (hereafter referred to as O'Neill.): Augustine, *A commentary on the New Code of Canon Law,* (8 volumes, 2 ed., St. Louis and London, 1918-1924.), I, p. 127.

the intermediary or executor, as he is termed by the Code.[27]

A favor that is granted *in forma gratiosa* is a favor that is granted directly by the grantor to the petitioner. There is no executor involved in the granting of a favor *in forma gratiosa.* A favor that is granted by this method becomes effective immediately upon its being conceded by the grantor, since no executor is required.[28]

It appears from the wording of canon 1138, §2, that a *sanatio in radice* is a favor that is granted either *in forma commissoria* or *in forma gratiosa.*[29]

A radical sanation, just as any other favor, depends upon the form of the rescript, and may be granted by either of the methods stated. Generally the favor, i.e., the convalidation, will be granted *in forma gratiosa* or *in forma commissoria* according to whether respectively the *sanatio in radice* is total or partial.

It may, perhaps, be said that generally a total sanation is granted *in forma gratiosa,* and a partial sanation *in forma commissoria,* because the incidents and circumstances accompanying the latter may well require something further to be done by the party or parties or by the executor, or ascertained by him, before the actual convalidation is effected.

It is the practice in many dioceses to always grant a radical sanation in *forma commissoria.* The local ordinary appoints the parish priest of the petitioner as the executor of the favor, so that the actual grant of the favor depends upon the prudent judgment of the parish priest. Since the parish priest is usually the person who requests the sanation in behalf of the petitioner, he is familiar with the case and therefore perhaps better qualified than anyone else to act as executor. Once the executor is satisfied that the proper required conditions are fulfilled, he requests the petitioner to sign a form accepting the radical sanation. The grant then becomes effective upon the signing of the form of acceptance. As it will be later treated (chapter III, article III, pp. 66 ff.), in a case involving either the impediment of mixed religion or the impediment of disparity of cult the bishop personally acts as executor of the favor.

---

[27] Canon 38: O'Neill, pp. 106 ff., 156.

[28] Cf. O'Neill, *loc cit.*

[29] "Convalidatio fit a momento concessionis gratiae."

Article IV. Differences between Simple Convalidation and *Sanatio in Radice*

Sanatio in Radice is primarily a means for the convalidation of a marriage itself[80] and as such it is one of two methods of convalidation that are established in the Code of Canon Law, the other method being simple convalidation.[81] A contrast of the differences of these two methods of convalidating previously invalid marriages, though this contrast be considered in general, will help to emphasize the uniqueness of the radical sanation.

Brennan defines simple convalidation as an act by which a marriage that has been null and void from the beginning is rendered valid through the renewal of consent.[82] Radical sanation as defined in canon 1138 §1 is the convalidation of a marriage carrying with it, besides the dispensation or cessation of the impediment, a dispensation from the law of the renewing of consent and the retroaction, through a fiction of law, of the canonical effects to the past.

Upon an examination of the definitions of these two types of convalidations it becomes apparent that the two have little in common. Both are methods of convalidating invalid marriages, but the means by which they achieve their purpose and the manner in which their effects are produced are quite different.[83]

In a simple convalidation the renewal of consent by the parties involved is absolutely necessary for validity, and no convalidation will be effected without it,[84] whereas in a radical sanation the convalidation carries with it a dispensation from the law requiring the renewal of consent.[85]

---

[80] Canon 1138.

[81] Canons 1133-1137.

[82] *Simple Convalidation of Marriage,* p. 2.

[83] Gasparri, *De Matrimonio,* II, 253 ff.: Wernz-Vidal, *Ius Matrimoniale,* pp. 851 ff.; Augustine, *A Commentary on Canon Law,* V, 380 ff.; Bouscaren-Ellis, *Canon Law,* pp. 575 ff.; Petrovits, *The New Church Law on Matrimony* (Philadelphia, 1921), pp. 424 ff.; Cappello, *De Sacramentis, V, De Matrimonio,* pp. 847 ff.; Coronata, *Tractaris & Sacramentis,* III, p. 934 ff.; Payen, *De Matrimonio in Missionibus,* II, 864 ff.; Brennan, pp. 3-5; Harrigan, Appendix I.

[84] Canon 1133.

[85] Canon 1138, §1.

If the marriage that is being convalidated is invalid owing to defect of form then in a simple convalidation that form must be observed.[36] On the other hand, in a *sanatio in radice* the convalidation is produced without any new observance of the form.[37] Should a marriage that is being convalidated be invalid because of the presence of a diriment impediment, a simple convalidation requires that when a dispensation from the impediment has been obtained it must be accompanied by a renewal of consent before the convalidation takes place.[38] A radical sanation, however, contains a dispensation not only from the impediment but also from the renewal of consent and the prescribed canonical form that attend the convalidation itself.[39] For marriages that are invalid because of defect of consent it is required in simple convalidation that the consent be supplied by one or both parties according to whether the consent is lacking on one or on both parts.[40] In a *sanatio in radice* a partial sanation may be granted if the consent was initially lacking but subsequently given. In such a case the partial sanation extends back to the point of time at which the consent was subsequently supplied. If the consent was never supplied and is still wanting at the time whence a convalidation is sought, no *sanatio in radice* may be had.[41]

These differences between a simple convalidation and a radical sanation have to do with the manner in which these two dispensations operate. In addition to the differences as regards their mode of operation there are also some striking dissimilarities in respect to the effects produced by these two methods of convalidation.

The two dispensations are identical in one respect; they serve to convalidate a previously invalid marriage. They differ noticeably in regard to the point of time at which the convalidation takes effect, however. The validation of a marriage by simple convalidation occurs at the time the consent is once more given according to canon 1081 but never before this new valid rendering of consent is had.[42] In

[36] Canon 1137.
[37] Canon 1138 §1.
[38] Canons 1133-1135.
[39] Canon 1138 §1.
[40] Canon 1136.
[41] Canon 1140.
[42] Canon 1133 §2.

sharp contrast a marriage is convalidated by a *sanatio in radice* from the moment the favor is granted by the competent authority.[43] The canonical effects of a marriage validated by simple convalidation are accorded to that marriage as effective from the time when the convalidation is produced as was stated above.[44] On the contrary, the canonical effects derived from a canvalidation through a radical sanation are effective retroactively, through a fiction of the law, to the beginning of the marriage unless the rescript should state otherwise.[45]

Simple convalidation and radical sanation also differ in the active or passive character that attaches to them in respect to the element of dispensation. In this contrast simple convalidation may be termed a passive dispensation, since the role that it plays in effecting validity to a marriage is rather a negative one. The active role in the giving of validity by simple convalidation is found not on the part of the dispensation, but rather in the role of the parties. If the marriage be invalid because of a diriment impediment the parties (or at least one of them) must petition for the dispensation to remove the impediment and then, the impediment having ceased, the parties, or at least the party conscious of the impediment, must renew consent according to the norms of canons 1133-1136. If the marriage is one that is invalid because of defect of form, it is required in a simple convalidation that the parties observe the prescribed form.[46] In this sense it is the parties, not the dispensation, who are supplying the activity.

Radical sanation is in direct contrast to simple convalidation in respect to the active or passive character attaching to the dispensation. Contrary to a simple canvalidation wherein the parties apply for the dispensation, a sanation may be granted apart from the knowledge of either party and therefore apart from their having applied,[47] and hence the parties may be completely passive as the radical sanation performs its task. The presence of a diriment impediment likewise requires *per se* no activity or applying for a dispensation by the parties, for such is the nature of the *sanatio* that the impediment is automatically dis-

[43] Canon 1138 §2.

[44] Canon 1116.

[45] Canon 1138 §1, §2.

[46] Canon 1137.

[47] Canon 1138 §3; Harrigan, pp. 77-78.

pensed concurrently with the granting of the radical sanation.[48] The renewal of consent by the parties, which is necessary for validity in a simple convalidation, is *per se* not required at all in a sanation, and accordingly as in the instance of the dispensation from the impediment, the parties remain passive while renewal of consent is *ipso facto* dispensed with as soon as the *sanatio in radice* is granted.[49]

Thus in contrasting simple convalidation with radical sanation, one may say that simple convalidation absolutely requires the active cooperation of the parties and so the dispensation is passive in character whereas radical sanation requires *per se* no active cooperation on behalf of the parties whatsoever, so that the *sanatio in radice* itself takes on an active quality. Perhaps the most striking example of how a radical sanation is active in respect to the favor and passive in respect to the parties is seen in the practice of the Holy See of granting sanations *in globo,* or general sanations as they are sometimes called, for a large group of people or even for an entire nation.[50] Many recipients of these sanations were totally passive thus not at all cognizant of the wonderful favor being granted to them in the grant of this extraordinary concession by Rome.

In making any comparison or contrast between simple convalidation and radical sanation it must be kept in mind that simple convalidation is the common, ordinary means of convalidating marriages and is to be used whenever possible. Radical sanation on the other hand is the rare, extraordinary means of convalidating marriages employed by the Church and as such is only to be used when it is not feasible or possible to have recourse to simple convalidation. This fact alone bears out the unique character of the *sanatio in radice.*

---

[48] Canon 1138 §1; cf. Harrigan, loc cit.

[49] Canon 1138 §1: But consent may be required under canon 1140. Cf. Harrigan, pp. 86, 87.

[50] Cf. supra p. 14 ff.

CHAPTER II

First Juridical Effect: The Convalidation of the Marriage

The juridic effects of a *sanatio in radice* are explicitly mentioned in canon 1138, §1, of the Code. So well defined and enumerated are these effects by the Code that one cannot add to or detract from any of the juridic effects as listed in canon 1138. The first juridic effect of a radical sanation that is listed by the Code is the convalidation of the previously invalid marriage. Since the writer intends to treat the effects in the order given in the Code, the convalidation of the marriage will be the first effect discussed.

In the previous chapter the writer treated the four juridic effects of a radical sanation according to their logical order. In that arrangement the convalidation of the marriage was preceded by both the dispensation from the impediment causing the invalidity of the marriage and the dispensation from the renewing of consent and was followed only by the retroactive concession of the canonical effects. However, the order of the effects given by the Code is according to import and in that order the convalidation of the marriage must be given preeminence.

When one breaks down and analyzes canon 1138 †1 into its component parts, which are the four juridic effects of the radical sanation, it could appear that each *sanatio in radice* produces four distinct effects. However, upon a closer examination of the grammatical construction employed in this canon it becomes apparent that it is not the mind of the legislator to imply that each sanation produces four distinct effects but on the contrary that the legislator is stressing the fact that each *sanatio in radice* is capable of producing one chief effect from which three additional effects inevitably flow. This seems to be the force of the use of *secumferens* by the legislator in canon 1138 §1.[1] Thus the chief juridic effect of a radical sanation is the convalidating of the previously invalid marriage while the three additional effects interwoven with the convalidation are (1) the dispensation from the impediment

1 "Matrimonii in radice sanatio est eiusdem convalidatio, secumferens, praeter dispensationem vel cessationem impedimenti, dispensationem a ledge de renovando consensu, et retroactionem, per fictionem iuris, circa effectus canonicos, ad preteritum."

causing the invalidity of the marriage, (2) the dispensation from the law of the renewing of consent, and (3) the retroaction of the canonical effects to the past.

Despite the dispensations, or negative elements, contained in a radical sanation, convalidation by a *sanatio in radice* is in reality something positive in nature. The grant of a radical sanation is in effect a declaration by the Church ratifying the true marital consent that the parties exchanged at the inception of their invalid union. This ratification is expressed in the dispensation from the law of the renewal of consent. In this third juridical effect of the *sanatio* the previously elicited and still continuing consent is accepted and ratified and the renewal of consent is dispensed with.[2]

Article I. Point of Time at Which Convalidation Takes Effect

In considering the point of time at which the convalidation takes its effect it should be explained that, although canon 1138 §1 deals with juridical effects that are regulated by the legislator in the Code of Canon Law, nevertheless there is an element in this canon that is above the juridic order. Marriage is truly a legal contract thereby falling under the general legislation regarding juridic contracts and the contract of matrimony in particular, but at the same time a marriage between two baptized persons is also a sacrament.[3]

The matrimonial contract itself between two baptized persons is a sacrament.[4] Therefore any legislation concerning the contractural element of such a marriage *ipso facto* also affects the sacramental element of marriage as well. This fact creates a major problem, since the sacramental order transcends the juridic order; and the difficulty created is of a very delicate nature. The difficulty precisely is this: that which effects matrimony is the exchange of consent by parties who are legally capable of contracting marriage with each other and this exchange of

[2] Wernz-Vidal, *Ius Matrimoniale*, n. 670; *infra*, p. 151.

[3] Canon 1012, §1; Council of Trent, Sess. XXIV, can. 1., *de matrimonio*. Schroeder, *Canons and Decrees of the Council of Trent Original Text with English Translation*, (Herder, St. Louis and London, 1941), p. 181.

[4] Canon 1012.

consent no human power is able to supply.[5] So in legislating concerning the marriage contract, the legislator must affect the sacramental and consensual elements of marriage, both of which are beyond his jurisdiction. This problem is very acute in the case of the *sanatio in radice,* for the legislator introduces an element of retroaction into the favor and, as canon 1081 so forcefully states, the consent of the parties most certainly does not come under the retroactive power of the legislator. The problem deals precisely with the moment of time when the convalidation should take place.

As regards the time element in the convalidation of a marriage by means of a radical sanation, the Code resolves the difficulty caused by the inseparability of the contractual and sacramental elements in marriage by using a precise juridic device termed a fiction of law.[6] This legal device enables the legislator to deal with the elements of a *sanatio in radice* in such a manner that he is able to remain within the scope of his power with respect to the sacramental element, which is not the object of the legal fiction. The convalidation of the marriage effected by a radical sanation occurs when the favor is granted by the Church,[7] and thus the convalidation itself is not affected by the retroactive power of the legislator. By use of a fiction of law the Code avoids any conflict between the sacramental and juridic orders in this sensitive situation, for the fiction of law is operative only in regard to the canonical effects of the marriage. The object and function of this *fictio iuris* will be explained in the final chapter.

The Code is so explicit in claiming that the convalidation of a marriage in a radical sanation takes effect only from the moment when the favor is conceded by the Church, that no one now may hold that the marriage itself is convalidated retroactively. To hold that the Church actually could sanate a marriage retroactively would be to attribute to it something that is entirely beyond the scope of its power, and which in fact is metaphysically impossible.[8]

---

5 Canon 1081.

6 Canon 1138 §1: "per fictionem iuris." This instrument of law is considered hereafter in connection with the canonical effects of radical sanation. Cf. Chapter V.

7 Canon 1138 §2: "Convalidatio fit a momento concessionis gratiae:".

8 Wernz-Vidal, Ius Matrimoniale, p. 850, footnote 12, "Nam ad praeterita non datur actio, atque facta infecta fieri non possunt."

That a marriage cannot be convalidated retroactively is a fact that now appears quite obvious to all. Despite this fact, however, many pre-code authors were of the opinion that the first and chief effect of a *sanatio in radice,* the convalidation, was really and truly granted retroactively.[9] This view of the pre-Code authors was refuted quite effectively by Pope Benedict XIV,[10] whose doctrine on the *sanatio in radice* today is still the basis for the juridical notions upon this subject.

Even though all modern day authors admit that the convalidation does not take effect retroactively or *ex tunc* but is effective only from the moment when the favor is granted or *ex nunc,* many of them still hold that the fiction of law applies also to the convalidation of the marriage as well as to the canonical effects. According to this view the convalidation takes effect at the moment that the favor is granted by the Church according to canon 1138 §2 but it is construed as though it were validated from the beginning of the marriage.

Harrigan seems to be of this opinion. However, he fluctuates in his work on *The Radical Sanation of Invalid Marriages* first treating of the union as though it were to be thought of as being valid from the time when the favor is granted, but then writing about the convalidation as though it were to be construed as valid *ab initio.* Finally he takes an unmistakable stand in the section that treats of the force of the convalidation.[11] Harrigan is not alone in his stand, for other authors supported the same view and apparently influenced him in formulating his decision.[12]

To dismiss this view as being unreasonable would be very rash, for the number of respected authors alone who have adopted this trend

---

9 Barbosa, *Vota,* Lib. II, votum XXVII, n. 1: Rigantius *Commentaria in Regulas* Tom. IV, Reg. L, n. 106; Perrone, *De Matrimonio Christiano,* II, pp. 147-152; Giovine, *De Dispensationibus Matrimonialibus,* I, consult. XXIII, sect. 23. Brillaud, *Traité Pratique des Dispenses de Mariage,* pp. 57, 279.

10 Const. *Etsi matrimonialis,* Sept. 27, 1755. *Bullarii Romani Continuatio Summorum Pontificum,* III, pars II, pp. 288-291.

11 "The Church cherishes, approves and confirms the juridical attitude that looks upon the newly convalidated marriage as if it had been valid from the beginning." Cf. p. 46 of his work.

12 Wernz-Vidal, *Ius Matrimoniale,* n. 670; Augustine, *A Commentary on Canon Law,* V, 391; Nau, *Manual on the Marriage Laws of the Code of Canon Law* (New York-Cincinnati, 1933), p. 212; Chelodi-Ciprotti, *De Matrimonio,* p. 211; Cappello, *De Sacramentis, V, De Matrimonio,* p. 858, n. 851.

of thought is sufficient evidence that it merits consideration. However, the writer is inclined to believe that the pre-Code tenor of thought influenced the modern authors a great deal in leading them to adopt this view, though canon 1138 §1 refers retroaction only to the canonical effects.

Certainly Gasparri in his pre-Code 1904 edition of *De Matrimonio* considerably impressed later authors who were to treat radical sanation. As president of the Code Commission any work of Gasparri's is very likely to be viewed as closest to the mind of the legislator, and this attitude is especially true since his work of 1904 pre-dated the Code by so few years. In this work Cardinal Gasparri has a text which undoubtedly has been interpreted as meaning that he holds that a marriage convalidated by a *sanatio in radice,* although being valid only *ex nunc,* is nevertherless looked upon as if it never had been invalid.[13] The 1904 edition of Wernz, a renowned pre-code authority, held that the fiction of law affected the convalidation as well as the canonical effects.[14] The writer believes that post Code authors were influenced more than a little by Wernz's and Gasparri's 1904 editions, and that they lean heavily upon the authority of the latter.

Another incident that perhaps may have influenced authors to claim that the fictitious retroactivity in a radical sanation pertained to the convalidation itself as well as to the canonical effects of the marriage was the wording used by a synod of the Oriental Church in 1898. An Egyptian Synod of Coptic Catholics so worded its description of a *sanatio in radice* that there was no doubt whatsoever as to the belief of the synod in regard to the fictitious retroaction as touching the marriage itself.[15]

Certainly the foregoing opinion is held by many respected authors and cannot be rejected without good cause. Despite the regard that

---

[13] Gasparri, *De Matrimonio* (1904 edit.), n. 1427. "Cum vero fingat dispensationem datam fuisse ante initas nuptias ac proinde matrimonium contractum fuisse sine impedimento ac ideo valium esse."

[14] Wernz, *Ius Decretalium,* IV, 970.

[15] *Synodus Alexandrina Coptorum Habita Cairi in Aegypto* (Romae, 1899.), p. 174, sectio secunda, art. VIII §7: "Ita ut matrimonium quod cum impedimento dirimente initum est ac proinde erat nullum hac sanatione considerandum est iuridice quasi celebratum fuerit absque hoc impedimento, ac ideo quasi fuerit ab initio validum."

the writer has for the authors endorsing this view, his opinion does not coincide with theirs. As a basis for holding that the retroaction through a fiction of law does not refer to the convalidation by a radical sanation but only to the canonical effects of the convalidated marriage, he advances the following arguments.

(1) The wording of the Code itself: the placing of the phrase "through a fiction of law" within the phrase dealing with the retroaction of the canonical effects to the past would seem to indicate that this retroaction refers to the canonical effects and to the canonical effects alone. The canon states that a sanation embodies the convalidation of the marriage, the dispensation from the impediment, the dispensation from the renewal of consent, and the retroaction, through a fiction of law, of the canonical effects to the past.[16] Now the retroaction of the canonical effects is only one of four separate favors contained in a radical sanation. And although the four favors are given together in the one grant by the Church, there is nothing in the wording of the Code to indicate, in the mind of the writer, that the retroaction by means of a fiction of law pertains to anything other than the canonical effects on the convalidated marriage. The writer holds that the Code does not imply that the convalidated marriage, though only valid *ex nunc,* is to be considered as though it always had been valid.

(2) The view of Cardinal Gasparri: As stated above it is the conviction of the writer that post Code authors treating of matrimony were greatly influenced by Cardinal Gasparri's 1904 canonical tract on marriage. Since this work was so closely followed by the formation and promulgation of the Code,[17] it can readily be seen, especially in view of the fact that Cardinal Gasparri became president of the Code Commission, how authors would accept his work as being expressive of the mind of the legislator. However, it must be remembered that despite the proximity of Cardinal Gasparri's work to the editing of the Code, his 1904 treatise was definitely pre-Code, and as such was subject to change with the promulgation of the Code. In 1932 Cardinal

[16] Canon 1138 §1, Matrimonii in radice sanatio est eiusdem convalidatio, secumferenes, prater dispensationem vel cessationem impedimenti, dispensationem a lege de renovando consensu, et retroactionem, per fictionem iuris, circa canonicus effectus, ad praeteritum

[17] The Code of Canon Law was promulgated on May 27, 1917.

Gasparri revised his *Tractatus Canonicus de Matrimonio,* deleting things that he thought were not in compliance with the Code. The including of the phrase *nova editio ad mentem Codicis Iuris Canonici* in the title of his 1932 edition bears out this purpose. It is noteworthy that in this 1932 work the text quoted previously[18] as showing that he held that a sanated marriage was to be considered as though it always had been valid is not to be found. In fact Cardinal Gasparri seemed to stress the fact that the marriage is convalidated *ex nunc* and nothing more, and hence that the consideration that a marriage convalidated by a radical sanation always had been valid is not implied in the Code.[19] The writer contends that Cardinal Gasparri changed his view, in accordance with the Code, on this matter in his 1932 edition, thus refuting his own 1904 text, which is cited as a proof by those espousing the opposite view, Coronata and Vermeersch-Creusen in their works appearing after Cardinal Gasparri's 1932 edition also fail to say that a marriage convalidated by a *sanatio in radice* is to be consutred as though it always had been valid.[20]

In addition to the two arguments listed above, the writer also adduces the following miscellaneous reasons as a support for his view that the Code does not imply that a marriage convalidated by a radical sanation is to be thought of as though it always had been valid. A supposed basis for the retroactive validity may be that since the canonical effects, which are admittedly the object of the retroaction in a *sanatio in radice* are the results of a marriage, it would seem only right to assume that these effects are the products of the marriage sanated. Therefore, since the effects are produced retroactively, the convalidated marriage must at least be construed as having been valid prior to the canonical effects because these effects result from the marriage. The writer rejects this assumption by making the following distinction between the sanated marriage and the retroactive effects. In a sanation the canonical effects are not in reality the results of the marriage: in a radical sanation these effects are produced retroactively through a fiction of law as though they had proceeded from a valid marriage. This result of the legal

---

18 Cf. *supra,* p. 51.

19 *De Matrimonio,* (nova editio, 1932), II, nn. 1208, 1209.

20 Cononata, *De Sacramentis* III (1946), n. 683; Vermeersch-Creusen, *Epitome Iuris Canonici,* II (6. ed., 1940), n. 455.

fiction does obviously not demand that this sanated marriage must be thought of as never having been invalid. The practice of the Church in granting imperfect sanations seems to justify this real distinction in fact and in law.[21]

An imperfect sanation may be granted in a case wherein one of the parties is deceased.[22] In this instance the canonical effects are bestowed retroactively, as though they had proceeded from a valid marriage. But the marriage bond of the parties itself is not affected: for with one of the parties deceased there is no bond to convalidate. Since there is no marriage present, the marriage obviously cannot be considered as being convalidated *ex tunc* since there is no question of convalidation at all.[23]

Another reason which the writer believes eliminates the cause for thinking of a sanated marriage as though it always had been valid is the lack of purpose for the retroactivity of the convalidation through a fiction of law. The purpose for the retroaction of the canonical effects is obvious, especially as regards the offspring who will profit from the retroactivity of these canonical effects.[24] However, the writer cannot envision any purpose in construing the sanated marriage as though it were valid from the very beginning of the union. The parties apparently have nothing to gain. The sacramental grace of matrimony cannot be granted retroactively; the marital right cannot be created retroactively; nor may any sins resulting from the invalid union be obliterated by a fiction of law. Thus the state of the parties seems to be none the worse because their marriage is to be considered and is, in fact, convalidated only as of the time when the Church grants the favor.

The writer then holds that a convalidation, i.e., a rendering the marriage valid by means of a *sanatio in radice,* is effective in concept and in fact only from the time when the Church grants the radical sanation according to canon 1138, §2, and that the retroaction involved in a sanation *in no way* refers to the convalidation of the union itself.

---

[21] E.g. the first radical sanation, cf. *supra,* p. 14.

[22] Wernz-Vidal, *Ius Matrimoniale,* n. 699.

[23] Wernz, *Ius Decretalium,* IV, 970; Harrigan, pp. 10, 11.

[24] Cf. *infra,* Chapter V.

Article II. Posthumous Granting of a *Sanatio in Radice*

Earlier in this work attention was given to the commonly accepted division of a *sanatio in radice,* i.e., perfect sanation and imperfect sanation which division is held by most modern authors.[25] In that section it was noted that an imperfect radical sanation is had if one or more of the effects of the sanation be lacking, or if each effect be not produced in its plenitude. On the surface this statement appears acceptable and free from difficulty; however, such is not the case. The problem raised by the accepted definition of an imperfect sanation is this: can a true radical sanation be granted if its first effects, namely the convalidation of the marriage, is wanting? Perhaps a better way of posing the problem would be as follows: can a true radical sanation be granted if it produces only the canonical effects of a convalidation as stated in canon 1138, §1, but not the convalidation itself?

The solution to this problem could appear to be obvious. A radical sanation of a marriage is primarily and essentially the convalidation of the marriage. Canon 1138, §1, leaves no doubt as to this statement.[26] Thus it might seem that no *sanatio,* perfect or imperfect, could be granted unless the convalidation of the marriage were effected also. The problem, however, does not admit to this simple answer. The main obstacle to this seemingly facile solution is derived from the history of the *sanatio in radice.*

The majority of authors, both pre-Code and post-Code, accept the first granting of a radical sanation as having occurred in the year 1301 and admit that sanations were granted apart from a convalidation being effected. Thus history obstructs a simple solving of the problem proposed above.[27] The first sanatio, however, was an imperfect sanation, or better perhaps, a sanation improperly so called.[28] The favor was

[25] Cf. *supra,* p. 4 ff.

[26] Matrimonii in radice sanatio est eiusdem convalidatio.

[27] Rigantius, *Commentaria in Regulas,* Tom, IV, Reg. XLIX, n. 11; Sanchez, *De Sancto Matrimonii Sacramento,* Lib. VIII, disp. VII, n. 6; Benedictus XIV, *Quaestiones Canonicae,* q. 174; Wernz-Vidal, *Ius Matrimoniale,* p. 863, Chelodi-Ciprotti, *De Matrimonio,* p. 212, n. 167; Coronata, *De Matrimonio,* p. 950, n. 685; Cappello, *De Sacramentis,* V, *De Matrimonio,* p. 857; Bouscaren-Ellis, *Canon Law,* p. 581; Gasparri, *De Matrimonio,* II, n. 1226; Petrovits, *The New Church Law on Matrimony,* p. 430, n. 596; Harrigan, p. 20.

[28] Harrigan, p. 11.

granted by Pope Boniface VIII to Maria, widow of Sancius IV, deceased King of Castille.[29] This sanation then did not convalidate the marriage, but produced only the effects of the marriage. Despite its common acceptance by authors the favor granted to Maria in 1301 does not conform to the definition of a *sanatio in radice* as expressed in canon 1138 §1. Modern authors vary in their explaining of this problem but their views may be reduced to two concepts.

Payen, Gasparri, and Bernhard espouse the first view. Payen explains the problem by saying that in a case wherein the canonical effects e.g. the legitimation of children, are produced, but owing to the death of one of the parties no convalidation is possible, then an improper sanation is had. This *sanatio* improperly so-called in the opinion of Payen imitates a true sanation, and is nothing more than the shadow of a true radical sanation.[30] Gasparri's view is very much like that of Payen. Gasparri admits that the Holy See is able to grant a *sanatio* when one of the parties is deceased, but he adds that in such an instance the favor granted is neither a true nor a proper sanation.[31] Jean Bernhard, contemporary French author, also holds with Payen and Gasparri that the retroactive granting of the canonical effects of the marriage independently of the convalidation, as is done when one of the parties is deceased, is not a true *sanatio in radice* according to the definition of a sanation given in canon 1138 §1.[32]

Cappello and Wernz-Vidal are the chief exponents of the second view, which teaches that the Holy See can grant a true *sanatio in radice,* even though one or both parties involved may have expired. Cappello holds that the Holy See not only can but actually does exercise this power, and the sanation granted is a true, though partial, *sanatio in radice.*[33] Wernz-Vidal likewise hold that a true sanation can be granted even in an instance where one or both of the parties are dead. According to Wernz-Vidal the grant of an imperfect sanation which

---

29 Cf. supra, p. 14.

30 *De Matrimonio in Missionibus,* II, n. 2607.

31 *De Matrimonio,* II, n. 1226.

32 "Propos sur la Natur Juridique de la 'sanatio in radice' dans le Droit Canonique Actuel," *Ephemerides Iuris Canonici,* IV, (1948) 394.

33 *De Sacramentis,* V, *De Matrimonio,* n. 850 bis, p. 857.

may be reduced to the conceding of the canonical effects of the marriage has no difficulty in itself.[34]

The writer holds the first view in this dispute, agreeing with Payen, Gasparri, and Bernhard, and rejecting the opinion of Cappello and Wernz-Vidal. The difficulty in this problem is chiefly one of terminology. The writer feels that, even though such authorities as Pope Benedict XIV and Sanchez applied the term *sanatio in radice* to the retroactive restoring of the canonical effects of a marriage in instances where death had destroyed the marriage bond, they did so for want of a better term to use, fully realizing that no true radical sanation was granted. The similarity between the retroactive restoring of the canonical effects along with the convalidation and the retroactive restoring of the canonical effects without the convalidation could explain why they adopted the term *sanatio* in the latter case. The writer feels that neither Sanchez nor Pope Benedict XIV intended to convey the idea that a true and strict *sanatio in radice* could be granted when there was no marriage bond to sanate.

Thus the writer sides with Payen, Gasparri, and Bernhard in holding that in cases wherein the canonical effects are granted apart from the convalidation of the marriage as happens when one or both of the parties are deceased, no true *sanatio in radice* is granted but only a sanation in the improper or wider sense of the term. Payen describes such a favor very adequately when he calls it a mere shadow of a true sanation.[35] As was stated above, the Code is quite explicit in saying that a radical sanation is the convalidation of a marriage. Hence, when no convalidation is effected, it is not possible to have a true sanation. To hold that a sanation may be had when there is no marriage bond to sanate, and thus no convalidation, appears contrary to canon 1138, §1, and any such view should be rejected.

Article III. Convalidation by Sanation in Cases of Insanity

Very similar to the question whether or not a true sanation can be granted in cases wherein death has destroyed the marriage bond is the

---

34 *Ius Matrimoniale,* p. 861, footnote 14.

35 *De Matrimonio in Missionibus,* II, n. 2607, "sed tamen non est nisi umbra verae sanationis."

query whether or not a *sanatio in radice* can be granted in an instance wherein one of the parties has fallen into complete and permanent insanity. Temporary insanity poses no problem, for in such a case it may be determined during a lucid interval or after the cessation of the insanity whether or not marital consent still endures. If it still continues then a radical sanation may be granted only during a lucid interval, convalidating the marriage and retroactively restoring the canonical effects of the marriage.[36]

Payen, Gasparri, Bernhard, DeSmet and Coronata[37] hold that the granting of a radical sanation in a case wherein one of the parties is permanently insane is identical with the granting of a sanation when death has destroyed the bond. In both instances no convalidation is effected for there is nothing to convalidate. On the one hand, death has destroyed the marital consent, while on the other hand total insanity has disrupted the continuance of the earlier given consent just as though the person had expired. In neither instance is convalidation possible. The bestowal of the canonical effects retroactively to a marriage where one of the parties is insane is nothing more than a sanation improperly so-called, not a true radical sanation, since it definitely does not fit the definition stated in canon 1138, §1, but is only a shadow or imitation of a true *sanatio*.

Cappello is of the view that not only may a true *sanatio in radice* be granted in an instance wherein complete insanity is present, but that this sanation actually convalidates the marriage since the marital consent still endures despite the insanity. Cappello admits that *de facto* the Church does not sanate marriages when one of the parties is insane, but he holds that theoretically the marriage could be convalidated. He teaches that the consent of the insane party still continues since it has never been revoked and that this consent is present in the insane person in the same manner as consent endures in a person who is sleeping or inebriated. Cappello claims that since one need not advert to one's consent to receive other sacraments, so one need not advert to one's

---

[36] Payen, *De Matrimonio in Missionibus,* II, n. 2615; Gasparri, *De Matrimonio,* II, n. 1222.

[37] Cf. footnotes 30, 31, 32; Coronata, *De Matrimonio,* p. 950; De Smet, *De Sponsalibus et Matrimonio,* II, 536.

consent as persevering in the case of the reception of a sanatio.[38] The crux of Cappello's argument seems to be whether or not permanent insanity destroys consent.

Once again the writer inclines toward the first view, holding with Payen, Gasparri, Bernhard, DeSmet, and Coronata that only an imitation of a true sanation or a *sanatio* improperly so-called can be granted when one of the parties is permanently insane. For the writer, permanent insanity is construed in the same manner as death in regard to a radical sanation, and hence no true sanation can ensue in this instance.

Cappello seems to base his argument for the granting of a true sanation on the idea that perpetual insanity does not destroy matrimonial consent. However, the writer cannot accept this doctrine. Matrimonial consent is an act of the will,[39] a deliberate human act that one permanently deprived of his sanity could not place. Now, if a person is permanently incapable of giving such consent it seems to the writer that such a person likewise cannot be said to persevere in the act of the will, even though he did place the act before lapsing into perpetual insanity. The writer must agree with the authors who are of the opinion that perpetual insanity dissolves matrimonial consent.[40] With the matrimonial consent dissolved there is no marriage to sanate and so a true *sanatio in radice* cannot be granted. Cappello in admitting that in practice the Holy See does not grant sanations in cases of permanent insanity cites a case to substantiate this admission.[41] This admission, even though it does not exclude the theoretical possibility of the Church's having the power to grant a sanation in such a case, certainly does not strengthen Cappello's argument. Cappello attempts to sustain his view by giving as an example the receiving of other sacraments by a person bereft of his reason. This example is not a legitimate comparison, however, for matrimony cannot be juridically considered in the same manner as the other sacraments. Matrimony besides being a sacrament, is a contract,[42] and so the consent to this contract is essen-

---

38 *De Sacramentis,* V, *De Matrimonio,* p. 862.

39 Canon 1081.

40 DeSmet, *op. cit.,* II, p. 536; Bernhard, *art. cit.,* p. 394; Coronata, *op. cit.,* p. 950; Payen, *op. cit.,* II, p. 905, n. 2607; Harrigan, p. 93.

41 *De Sacramentis,* V, *De Matrimonio,* p. 863; footnoe 16.

42 Canon 1012.

tial to the valid reception of the sacrament. Thus one may not legitimately reason that, in as much as an insane person may validly receive baptism, he can by the same token validly contract matrimony, for there is no juridic parity between the two sacraments. The fact that a person who is sleeping or inebriated may be the recipient of a sanation does not justify the claim that a permanently insane person likewise may receive a sanation, for in the one instance consent perseveres, though it be temporarily passive, while in the latter case the continuance of consent has been dissolved. In view of these objections to Cappello's view, the writer feels justified in saying that a true *sanatio in radice* cannot be granted if one of the parties involved has fallen prey to permanent insanity.

CHAPTER III

Second Juridical Effect: The Dispensation from the Impediment

The second juridical effect of a *sanatio in radice* is the dispensation from the impediment that caused the invalidity of the marriage.[1] As was mentioned in Chapter 1, the dispensation from the impediment is the first favor granted in a radical sanation if the logical order of the effects is followed. The dispensing from the renewing of consent, the convalidation itself of the marriage, and the retroactive producing of the canonical effects to the past all require that the impediment causing the invalidity of the marriage contract first be removed. After the impediment is dispensed by the Church, the other favors contained in a radical sanation become operative.

An impediment may strictly be defined as a circumstance attaching to the person which according to law renders his marriage illicit or invalid.[2] Impediments may be either of the divine or of the ecclesiastical law, according to the source whence they arise. They are termed either impedient or diriment impediments according to whether they render the marriage illicit or invalid, respectively.[3] Impedient impediments[4] are of no concern to the writer in this work, for a marriage that is illicit but valid cannot be the object of a *sanatio in radice.* The second juridical effect of sanation has reference only to a dispensation from a diriment impediment since it is this type of impediment that renders a marriage the possible object of a subsequent radical sanation.

Whether the diriment impediment arises from the divine or from the ecclesiastical law is of great import in the petitioning for a *sanatio in radice.* In view of this importance the writer will give special attention to the origin whence the diriment impedient arises. First he will treat the impediments of the positive or natural divine law, and, then impediments of the purely ecclesiastical law.

---

[1] Canon 1138 §1.

[2] Bouscaren-Ellis, *Canon Law,* p. 482.

[3] Canon 1036.

[4] With the exception of mixed religion, cf. p. 66.

Article I. Impediments of the Positive or Natural Divine Law

The diriment matrimonial impediments of the divine positive or the natural law cannot be dispensed by any human authority or even by the Church.[5] Impediments of this type are few, very probably being but three in number. The impediment of an existing bond of marriage (*ligamen*) is a diriment impediment of the positive divine law; antecedent and perpetual impotence and consanguinity in the first degree of the direct line are diriment impediments of the natural law.[6]

The question whether or not the Holy See has the power to grant a radical sanation in the case of a marriage invalidated by a diriment impediment of the positive or natural divine law has long been a point of disputation among canonists. The dispute concerns not whether the Holy See san dispense directly from an impediment of the positive or natural divine law, since it is obvious that no human authority has the power to do so, but rather whether or not the Holy See has the power to grant a *sanatio in radice* after such impediment invalidating the marriage has ceased to exist.

Pope Benedict XIV in treating radical sanation stated that a sanation cannot be granted in the case of an impediment of the divine law.[7] Sanchez went so far as to hold that in the case of a doubt whether or not the impediment was of the divine law the Holy Father should not refrain from dispensing.[8] Gasparri rejected this view and stated that in such a doubt the Pope should never exercise his power of dispensing.[9] Consanguinity in the direct line in degrees other than the first, and consanguinity in the first degree of the collateral line (brother-sister) are doubtful impediments of the natural law. Because of this *dubium* that exists it is the practice of the Church never to dispense from these impediments.[10]

---

[5] Gasparri, *De Matrimonio,* I, n. 263; Wernz-Vidal, *Ius Matrimoniale,* n. 407.

[6] Noldin-Schmitt, *Summa Theologiae Moralis,* III, n. 554. But concerning consanguinity Noldin's classification is too narrow, cf. *infra,* p. 62.

[7] *Quaestiones Canonicae,* q. 174.

[8] *De Sancto Matrimonii Sacramento,* Lib. III, lib. VIII, n. 10.

[9] *De Matrimonio,* I, n. 263.

[10] Canon 1076 §3 "Nunquam matrimonium permittatur, si quod subsit dubium num partes sint consanguineae in aliquo gradu lineae rectae aut in primo gradu lineae collateralis." G. Gasparri, *De Matrimonio,* I, n. 712; Cap-

The fact that the Pope has the power to dispense from conditional provisions of the divine law[11] should not be interpreted as meaning that in such an instance the Pope is dispensing from the positive divine law itself, for such is not the case. The Holy Father is relaxing the human act which brought the person under the positive divine law.[12]

The dispute then concerns not whether a perfect radical sanation can be granted in the case of a marriage invalid by an impediment of the positive or natural divine law, even though of doubtful natural law origin, since that is impossible, or in the latter instance certainly not to be expected, but whether an imperfect *sanatio in radice* can be given. The imperfect *sanatio in radice* would grant the canonical effects of the marriage retroactive at least to the point at which the impediment ceased to exist. Prior to the promulgation of the Code the dispute was one of practical importance and it involved some of the leading pre-Code authorities.[13] However, the Code reduced the dispute to one of speculative value, for while avoiding the issue as to whether or not the Holy See can grant a sanation in this instance, it does determine quite plainly that the Church does not sanate marriages contracted with an impediment of the positive or natural divine law even though the impediment has ceased.[14]

Cardinal Gasparri was one of the leading exponents for the affirma-

---

pello, *De Matrimonio,* n. 518; Wahl, *Consanguinity and Affiity,* The Catholic University of America Canon Law Studies, n. 90, (Catholic University of America, Washington, D.C., 1934.), pp. 28, 29.

[11] I.e. provisions that depend upon the free will of man, v.b. vow, *ratum et non-consummatum* marriage of the faithful, consummated marriage of infidels; Gasparri, *De Matrimonio,* I, n. 263; Harrigan, p. 97.

[12] Bouscaren-Ellis, *Canon Law,* pp. 489, 490.

[13] Cf. *supra,* p. 27; Wernz-Vidal, *Ius Matrimoniale,* n. 663; footnote 25; Cappello, *De Sacramentis,* V, *De Matrimonio,* n. 854; Gasparri, *De Matrimonio,* II, nn. 1216-1219.

[14] Canon 1139 §2. Matrimonium vero contractum cum impedimento iuris naturalis vel divini, etiamsi postea impedimentum cessaverit, Ecclesia non sanat in radice, ne a momento quidem cessationis impediment. As to these impediments cf. Reiffenstuel, *Ius Canonicum Universum, append.* ad lib IV, cap 1, n. 7; Noldin-Schmitt, *Summa Theologiae Moralis,* III, n. 554; canon 1076 §3; canon 1038 §1; Fang, *Dispensatio Matrimonialis,* (Romae, *Officium Libri Catholici,* 1946.), pp. 102-103, 106-108; O'Keeffe, *Matrimonial Dispensations,* p. 218; Wahl, *Consanguinity and Affinity,* pp. 28, 29.

tive view in this argument. Even after the Holy Office declared in favor of the negative view in 1904,[15] he continued to uphold the power of the Church to grant radical sanations under such circumstances. Cardinal Gasparri stated that as President of the Code Commission, it was he who prevailed upon Pope Pius X, who already had approved the response, not to include the response of 1904 of the Holy Office in the Code. Gasparri argued that such a move would give dogmatic value to the response and would deny definitely the power of the Holy See to exercise the power of sanation in such cases. Gasparri and his adherents carried their point, and when the issue was introduced into the Code, it was changed from "cannot sanate" to "does not sanate."[16]

The affirmative view held by Gasparri and other post Code canonists is the view adopted by the writer.[17] The affirmative view, in the mind of the writer, seems to be logically deducible from the legislation in the Code. It is granted that the Church cannot dispense from impediments of the positive or natural divine law. However, once the impediment has ceased, there appears to be no reason why the Church cannot grant an imperfect *sanatio in radice.* There now is no impediment obstructing the validity of the marriage, and there is no need for a renewal of consent, since the consent first exchanged by the parties is presumed to persevere despite the fact that the union was initially entered into invalidly owing to the presence of a diriment impediment.[18] Also there is no reason present why the canonical effects cannot be granted retroactively to the point of time at which the impediment ceased, since the consent was present at that moment and the circumstances do not seem to differ substantially from those envisioned

---

[15] S.C.S. Off., 2 mart. 1904. "Matrimonium contractum cum impedimento iuris naturalis vel divini non posse sanari in radice." (*Collect. S.C. de Prog. Fide,* II, n. 2188.

[16] Gasparri, *De Matrimonio,* II, nn. 1217, 1218.

[17] Gasparri, *De Matrimonio,* II, nn. 1217, 1218; Cappello, *De Sacramentis,* V, *De Matrimonio,* n. 854, Wernz-Vidal, *Ius Matrimoniale,* n. 850; Chelodi-Ciprotti, *De Matrimonio,* n. 168.

[18] Canon 1093. Etsi matrimonium invalide ratione impedimenti initum fuerit, consensus praestitus praesiumitur perseverare, donec de cius revocations constiterit.

in canon 1140, §2.[19] The Code itself appears to support the affirmative view, since the law says explicitly *does not sanate,* and not *is not able to sanate.*

The Church has in fact granted an imperfect sanation for a marriage that was entered into invalidly because of the presence of the impediment of a previously existing bond of marriage, diriment impediment of positive divine law. The Sacred Penitentiary issued a response on April 25, 1890, that sanated a marriage entered into invalidly because of the impediment of ligamen and in this case the effects were granted retroactively to the time that the impediment ceased. No renewal of consent was demanded because the initial exchange of consent was deemed to have persevered. The children who had been born of the union were made legitimate with the exception of the offspring conceived in adultery. Gasparri stated that, notwithstanding the response of the Holy Office in 1904 and the wording of canon 1139, §2, the Holy Office and other Sacred Congregations in the external forum and the Sacred Penitentiary in the internal forum will grant an imperfect sanation for marriages invalidated by impediments of the divine law, provided, of course, the impediment has ceased and that there are extremely serious causes for the *sanatio in radice.*[20]

In consideration of the positive points in favor of the affirmative view, the writer holds that the Holy See has the power to grant an imperfect radical sanation for a marriage invalidated by an impediment of the positive or natural divine law, provided that the impediment has ceased, and to cause the retroactivity of the canonical effects to extend back to the time of the cessation of this impediment. The perseverance of the consent naturally is a requisite for such a grant by the Holy See.

Article II. Impediments of the Ecclesiastical Law in General

The diriment impediments of the ecclesiastical law that render a marriage invalid are the following: lack of canonical age[21] disparity of

---

[19] "Quod si consensus ab initio quidem defuerit, sed postea praestitus fuerit, sanatio concedi potest a momento praestiti consensus."

[20] *De Matrimonio,* II, n. 1219.

[21] Canon 1067; [22] Canon 1070; [23] Canon 1072.

cult,[22] Sacred Order,[23] solemn religious vow,[24] abduction,[25] crime,[26] consanguinity,[27] affinity,[28] public propriety,[29] spiritual relationship,[30] and adoption if in the civil law itself this relationship invalidates marriage.[31] The impediment of disparity of cult together with that of mixed religion will be treated separately in the article immediately following.

There is no problem concerning the power of the Church to grant radical sanations for marriages invalid because of diriment impediments of merely ecclesiastical law. The Apostolic See has the exclusive right to establish diriment impediments of the ecclesiastical law,[32] and it alone has the power to abrogate them or derogate from them.[33] Since the Holy See is the legislator in the establishing of these invalidating impediments, the Holy See can dispense from them. The same power that enables a legislator to make laws enables the legislator to dispense from those same laws.[34] Canon 1139 §1 makes it rather clear that any marriage invalid because of a diriment impediment of the ecclesiastical law can be sanated provided, of course, that the consent perseveres.[35]

Despite the fact that the Church has the power to dispense from all impediments of the ecclesiastical law, there are some impediments from which the Church is not wont to dispense. The impediment of Sacred Order in regard to the priesthood and episcopate is an ecclesiastical impediment that was rarely dispensed in the past and is never dispensed according to the present practice of the Holy See.[36]

[24] Canon 1073; [25] Canon 1074; [26] Canon 1075; [27] Canon 1076, i.e., consanguinity other than the direct line and the first degree of the collateral line, cf. p. 46a.

[28] Canon 1077; [29] Canon 1078; [30] Canon 1079.

[31] Canon 1080.

[32] Canon 1038 §2.

alone has the power to abrogate them or derogate from them.[33] Since

[33] Canon 1040.

[34] Canon 80.

[35] "Quodlibet matrimonium initum cum utriusque partis consensu naturaliter sufficiente, sed iuridice inefficaci ob dirimens impedimentum iuris ecclesiastici vel ob defectum legitimae formae, potest in radice sanari, dummodo consensus perseveret."

[36] Garcia-Bayon, *Tractatus Canonico-Moralis de Sacramento Matrimonii*, (2 vols., Madrid, 1931.) I, n. 358; Harrigan, p. 101; O'Keeffe, *Matrimonial Dispensations*, p. 219; Gasparri, *De Matrimonio*, I, nn. 618, 619; Cappello, *De Sacramentis, V, De Matrimonio*, n. 442; Wernz-Vidal, *Ius Matrimoniale*, n.

Another such impediment of the ecclesiastical law that is not the object of a dispensation is the impediment of affinity in the direct line after the marriage giving rise to the impediment has been consummated.[37] The fact that these two impediments are omitted from all grants of faculties given by the Holy See and are excluded from the extraordinary concession of faculties contained in canons 1043, 1044, and 1045 exemplifies the fact that the Holy See has chosen not to grant dispensations from those impediments.

Besides the two impediments of the ecclesiastical law, i.e., sacred priesthood and affinity in the direct line once the marriage has been consummated, from which the Holy See regularly does not dispense, there are other impediments of the ecclesiastical law, which ordinarily are not the object of a dispensation for the purpose of contracting marriage. According to O'Keeffe these impediments are the lack of canonical age, Sacred Order (beneath the priesthood), solemn vow, abduction, and the public crime of conjugicide.[38] However, Harrigan adds "But once a marriage has been contracted invalidly because of these and other merely ecclesiastical impediments, excepting (reguarly) priesthood and affinity in the direct line (the marriage having been consummated), the Church dispenses from these impediments more readily in order to procure the convalidation of the marriage."[39] Even

228; Decree of the Sacred Penitentiary, April 18, 1936, *AAS* XVIII, 1936, p. 242; Bouscaren, *The Canon Law Digest,* (2 vols., and Supplement, through 1948, Bruce, Milwaukee.), II, 579: "The law of sacred celibacy for the Latin clergy has always been and is now so treasured by the Church that, in the case of priests, dispensation from it, in past times, was hardly ever granted, and according to present discipline is never given, not even in danger of death." Translation of a pertinent passage in the *AAS* in the volume and on the page here cited.

[37] Harrigan, p. 101; O'Keeffe, *Matrimonial Dispensations,* p. 219; Vermeersch-Creusen, *Epitome Iuris Canonici,* II, n. 358; Gasparri, *De Matrimonio,* I, n. 722; Wernz-Vidal, *Ius Matrimoniale,* n. 370; Cappello, *De Sacramentis, V, De Matrimonio,* n. 529.

[38] *Matrimonial Dispensations,* p. 220; Pontificia Commissio ad Codicis Canones authentice Interpretandas, (CPI), 26 ian. 1949: "D. I. An sub verbis can. 81 'a generalibus Ecclesiae legibus' comprehendantur vota Sedi Apostolicae reservata. D. II. An Ordinarii, vi can. 81 et sub clausulis in eo recensitis, valeant dispensare subdiaconos et diaconos ab obligatione servandi sacrum caelibatum. R. Negative ad utrumque."—*AAS,* XLI (1949), 158.

[39] *The Radical Sanation of Invalid Marriages,* p. 102.

though it is the practice of the Church not to dispense from the impediment of affinity in the direct line once the marriage has been consummated, Gasparri stated that on rare occasions for very grave reasons this dispensation is granted.[40] In the case of the impediment of consanguinity in the first degree of the collateral line mixed with the second (uncle-niece, aunt-nephew) the Holy See is reluctant to grant the dispensation unless there are proportionately grave canonical causes present. In regard to this matter a grave instruction urging Ordinaries to restrain their subjects from requesting this dispensation and advising them not to seek the dispensation unless the valid and grave canonical causes were present was issued by the Sacred Congregation of the Sacraments on August 1, 1931.[41]

Hence with the practice of the Church as a guide the following may be said: although the Holy See does not encourage petitions for radical sanations of marriages invalid because of one of the above mentioned impediments, the *sanatio* will be granted if proportionately grave reasons dictate its concession, and if there appears to be no other way of procuring a convalidation. The reluctance of the Church to grant a dispensation from one of the ecclesiastical impediments listed by O'Keeffe[42] for the purpose of contracting marriage indicates that the Church is more likely to dispense from one of these matrimonial impediments *post factum* in a *sanatio in radice* than She is *ante factum.*[43]

Article III. Impediments of Disparity of Cult and Mixed Religion

Another matter of which notice must be taken here is the radical sanation of an attempted marriage that is invalid because it is contracted before a civil official or non-Catholic minister in the face of the diriment impediment of disparity of cult or the impedient impediment of mixed religion. Aside from other practical considerations that invalid marriages contracted in the face of the diriment impediment of disparity of cult and impedient impediment of mixed religion have in

[40] *De Matrimonio,* I, n. 722, p. 443; II, n. 1218. For a brief discussion of causes cf. *op. cit.,* I, n, 722, p. 443.

[41] *AAS,* XXIII (1931), 413; Bouscaren, *Canon Law Digest,* I, 514.

[42] Cf. *supra,* p. 35.

[43] Harrigan, pp. 101, 102.

common, they both require in their convalidation the fundamental guarantee that assures for future progeny their baptism in the Catholic Faith and their exclusive rearing in the same Catholic Faith.[44]

Disparity of cult is a diriment impediment of the ecclesiastical law[45] and hence its presence prevents the contracting of a valid marriage. In addition to this fact, both the impediment of disparity of cult and the impediment of mixed religion are impedient impediments of the divine law when there is present the danger of religious perversion of the Catholic consort and the offspring.[46] This prohibition of the divine law, which is not subject to the ecclesiastical authority of dispensing,[47] calls for essential consideration in the Church's dealing with either the impediment of disparity of cult or the impediment of mixed religion as an ecclesiastical impediment in relation to the grant of a *sanatio in radice*. These cases of invalid marriages are amenable to convalidation by means of radical sanation, provided that the danger to the Catholic Faith of the Catholic party and of the children is removed according to the mind of the Holy See.[48] Marriages that are invalid in the face of the impediment of disparity of cult or the impediment of mixed religion lack validity by reason of the ecclesiastical law. Since it is apparent that the church can, and does, convalidate marriages invalid because of the ecclesiastical law,[49] attention now will be given to these two impediments in connection with the Diocesan Quinquennial Faculties. It must be noted before proceeding further that the Holy See delegates the power to sanate marriages invalid in the face of either the impediment of disparity of cult or the impediment of mixed religion only when these said marriages are attempted before a civil magistrate or a non-Catholic minister. Marriages invalid because of defect

---

[44] Canons 1061, 1071.

[45] Canon 1070; *supra*, p. 65; Bouscaren-Ellis, *Canon* Law, p. 532.

[46] Canons 1060, 1071; for a brief description of the *periculum perversionis* cf. *infra*, p. 74.

[47] Cappello, *De Sacramentis*, V, *De Matrimonio*, n. 309, §1; Gasparri, *De Matrimonio*, I, n. 263; Wernz-Vidal, *Ius Matrimoniale*, n. 407; *Instructio S.C.S. Officii*, Feb. 1, 1871: "Conditiones omnino necessariae, quae ideo in promiscuis nuptiis requiruntur, quia in naturali ac divino iure fundantur, huiusmodi sunt, quea remitti seu dispensari numquam possunt."—*Fontes*, n. 1013.

[48] Canons 1061-1064.

[49] Canon 1139, §1; *supra*, c. III, art. II.

of form only or invalid because of the impediment of disparity of cult (though *coram ecclesia*) cannot be sanated in virtue of the Quinquennial Faculties.

The Holy Office is the Sacred Congregation competent to sanate a marriage contracted before a civil official or non-Catholic minister invalidly under the accompaniment of the impediment of disparity of cult or also the impediment of mixed religion.[50] The faculty of sanating these marriages has also been delagated according to the terms of the grant to the various ordinaries by the Holy Office.[51] The terms of this grant serve to reveal, at least in a definite measure, the mind of the Holy See with reference to the absence or the removal of any prohibition of the divine law latent in any particular cases. Under this aspect only are the faculties here considered. It is outside the scope of this work to present a commentary on these faculties.[52]

The text of the quinquennial faculties for the granting of a *sanatio in radice* in these cases is the following:

"Sanandi in radice matrimonia attentata coram officiali civili vel ministro acatholico a suis subditis etiam extra territorium, aut non subditis, intra limites proprii territorii, cum impedimento mixtae religionis aut disparitatis cultus, dummodo consensus in utroque coniuge perseveret, isque legitime renovari non possit, sive quia pars acatholica de invalidate matrimonii moneri nequeat sine periculo gravis damni aut incommodi a catholico coniuge subeundi; sive quia pars acatholica ad renovandum coram Ecclesia matrimonialem consensum, aut ad cautiones praestandas, ad praescriptum Cod. I. C. can. 1061, §2, ullo modo induci nequeat; dummodo;

1°—moraliter certum sit patrem acatholicam non esse impedituram baptismum et catholicam educationem universae prolis forte nasciturae;

2°—pars catholica explicite promittat se, pro posse, curaturam esse baptismum et catholicam educationem universae prolis forte

---

[50] Canon 247; *supra*, p. —; Harrigan, pp. 120, 121.

[51] Eagleton, *The Diocesan Quinquennial Faculties, Formula IV*, (The Catholic University of America Press, Washington, D.C., 1948), p. 61; Beste, Introductio in Codicem, Allegatum I, n. 4.

[52] Cf. Eagleton, *The Diocesan Quinquennial Faculties, Formula IV*, for such a commentary.

nasciturae, et (si casus ferat) etiam conversionem, baptismum, catholicam educationem prolis iam natae;

3°—partes, ante attentatum matrimonium, sive privatim sive per publicum actum, se non obstrinxerint ad educationem acatholicam prolis;

4°—neutra pars sit actu demens;

5°—pars saltem catholica sit sanationis conscia eamque petat;

6°—nullum aliud obstet canonicum impedimentum dirimens, super quo Ipse Ordinarius dispensandi aut sanandi facultate non polleat.

"Ipse autem excmus Episcopus R.P.D. serio moneat partem catholicam de gravissimo patrato scelere, salutares ei poenitentias imponat et, si casus ferat, eam ab excommunicatione absolvat iuxta C.I.C. can. 2319, §1, simulque declaret ob sanationis gratiam a se acceptam, matriomium effectum esse validum, legitimum et indissolubile iure divino, et prolem forte susceptam vel suscipiendam, legitmam esse; eique insuper in mentem revocet obligationem qua tenetur proudenter curandi conversionem coniugis ad fidem catholicam.

"Cum autem de matrimonii validitate et prolis legitimatione in foro externo constare debeat, Excmus R.P.D. Episcopus mandet ut singulis vicibus documentum sanationis cum attestatione peractae executionnis diligenter custodiatur in Curia locali, nec non curet, nisi pro sua prudentia aliter iudicaverit, ut in libro baptizatorum paroechiae, ubi pars catholica baptismum recepit, transcribatur notitia sanationis matrimonii, de quo actum est, cum adnotatione diei er anni."

"Mens autem S. Officii est ut Episcopus hanc facultatem sanandi matrimonia in radice per se ipse personaliter exerceat, scilicet nemini subdeleget."[58]

The quinquennial faculties give to the ordinary the power of radically sanating marriages that were attempted either before a civil official or a non-Catholic minister. The power is applicable to the subjects of the ordinary even outside the confines of the diocese, and to those who are not his subjects within the limits of the diocese. The consent must

[58] Effective January 1, 1954; Sacra Congregatio Consistorialis: *Index Facultatum Quinquennalium Ordinariis Locorum Tributarum, Formula IV.*

persevere in each party and there must be a legitimate reason why the consent can not in due form be renewed. This circumstance may be present because the non-Catholic party cannot be advised of the invalidity of the marriage without danger of grave harm or serious inconvenience to the Catholic party, or because the non-Catholic party cannot be induced in any way to renew his consent before the Church or to officially make the otherwise required guarantee (*cautiones*). The foregoing concession depends upon the verification of the following conditions:

1—that there be moral certitude that the non-Catholic party will not impede the baptism and the Catholic education of any of the children to be born of the union;[54]

2—that the Catholic party promise that he will, insofar as he is able, bring about the baptism and Catholic education of all the children to be born of the union ,and, if the situation allows it, the conversion, the baptism, and the Catholic education of the children already born of the union;

3—that the parties did not before their attempted marriage, bind themselves, by either a private or public act, to the non-Catholic education of the children;

4—that neither of the parties be insane;

5—that at least the Catholic party know of the sanation and seek it;

6—that there exist no other diriment impediment with reference to which the ordinary lacks the power of dispensing or sanating.

The ordinary is instructed in the faculties to seriously admonish the Catholic party concerning the grave crime committed, to impose upon him a salutary penance and, if the occasion demands it, to absolve him, according to canon 2319, §1, from the excommunication incurred. At the same time the ordinary is to declare that by reason of the favor of the radical sanation received from him the marriage is valid, legitimate, and indissoluble by divine law, and that the children already born and also those yet to be born are legitimate. Moreover, the ordinary is to refresh in the mind of the Catholic party the obligation of endeavoring prudently to effect the conversion of the non-Catholic spouse to the Catholic Faith.

Since the convalidation of the marriage and the legitimation of

[54] Cf. Bouscaren, *Canon Law Digest,* Supplement through 1948, p. 12, note 3.

the offspring are to be established in the external forum, the ordinary should demand that in each case the document of the sanation together with the attestation of its execution is to be diligently filed in the diocesan curia, and that, unless he prudently judge otherwise, the fact of the sanation and the date of its concession should be inscribed in the baptismal registry of the parish where the Catholic party received baptism.

The faculty explicitly states that it is the mind of the Holy Office that the bishop personally execute this faculty of sanating, not subdelegating the power to any one. Since there is no reservation of this faculty to the bishop alone, the word bishop may be construed as referring also to the vicar general.[55]

Although the non-Catholic is, in effect, not required by this document to furnish the explicit *cautiones* that juridically and formally are demanded by canon 1061,[56] the moral certitude as it is demanded in the first of the six conditions listed in the quinquennial faculties in some measure offsets, so it seems, the disadvantage of the non-giving of these *cautiones* in writing or explicitly by word of mouth, though they should be obtained when within reason that remains possible. In much the same manner the fulfilling of the first three conditions, along with the personal execution of the favor by the bishop, indicates the care exercised by the Church when expressing its mind that the *periculum* of canon 1066 be removed before a *sanatio in radice* be granted.

When the Church modifies the formal requirements of the *cautiones* according to canon 1061, it is not dispensing from the divine law. The fact that *cautiones* are required is as such a matter of ecclesiastical origin, although they are demanded in view of the divine law's prohibition in the face of the *periculum perversionis*. The *cautiones* are safeguards or guarantees obtained by the Church in token of the non-viola-

---

[55] Canon 368, §2; Eagleton, *Diocesan Quinquennial Faculties, Formula IV*, p. 68; cf. Bouscaren, *Canon Law Digest*, I, 64.

[56] §1. "Ecclesia super impedimento mixtae religionis non dispensat nisi:

1°. Urgeant iustae ac graves causae:

2°. Cautionem praestiterit coniux acatholicus de amovendo a congiue catholico perversionis periculo, et uterque coniux de universa prole catholice tantum baptizanda et educanda;

3°. Moralis habeatur certitudo de cautionum implemento.

§2. Cautiones regulariter in scriptis exigantur.

tion of the divine law through the contracting of mixed marriages. If in a given instance the Church believes that the Faith of the Catholic party and of the offspring is not in danger, or that the danger is absent even apart from the *cautiones*, then the Church can modify the measure of its normal safeguards, inasmuch as they are not required in the case. This point is explained very well by Schenk in his study of mixed religion and disparity of cult.[57]

The *periculum* to which canon 1060 specifically adverts is the danger to the Faith of the Catholic party and the offspring. This danger gives rise to a prohibition of the divine law,[58] for in the threat to the Faith of the Catholic party there lurks also the threat to the eternal salvation of his soul. To allow a party to enter a mixed marriage when he is unprepared for neutralizing the proximate dangers to his eternal salvation that may await him would certainly be opposed to the salvific will of God, who desires all men to be saved.[59] Pope Leo XIII (1878-1903), when stressing the dangers involved in mixed marriages, quite vividly listed the particular evils and showed why the *periculum* mentioned in canon 1060 is outlawed by the divine law itself. In speaking of these marriages, Leo XIII stated that, when minds disagree concerning the observance of religion, it is scarcely possible to expect agreement on other matters. Persons should dread mixed marriages, for they give occasion to forbidden association and communion in religious matters; threaten the Faith of the Catholic party; hinder the proper education of the offspring; and often lead to a confusing of truth and falsehood that culminates in the belief that one religion is as good as another.[60] This statement of Pope Leo XIII clearly gives

---

[57] *The Matrimonial Impediments of Mixed Religion and Disparity of Cult*, The Catholic University of America, Washington, D.C., 1929, pp. 174-179, 214, 215.

[58] Exodus, XXXIV, 16; Deut., VII, 1-4; I Cor., VII, 39; II Cor., VI, 14; Gasparri, *De Matrimonio*, I, n. 439; Schenk, *The Matrimonial Impediments of Mixed Religion and Disparity of Cult*, pp. 8, 9.

[59] I Timothy, III, 2-4.

[60] Ep. encycl *Arcanum*, 10 Febr. 1880, n. 26: ". . . animos enim de disciplina religionis dissidentes vix sperari potest futuros esse cetera concordes. Quin imo ab eiusmodi coniugiis ex eo maxime persicitur esse abhorrendum, quod occasionem praebent vetitae societati et communicationi rerum sacrarum, periculum religioni creant coniugis catholici, impedimento sunt bonae institutioni

No matter what precautions are taken to protect the Faith of a Catholic party entering a mixed marriage, it does not seem possible to remove absolutely the *periculum perversionis.* However, if the guarantees and safeguards envisioned in canons 1061 and 1062 are fulfilled, the *periculum* can be rendered so remote that it is practically non-existent in this particular case. The *periculum* may be made remote if the following conditions are present: 1— the non-Catholic party does not interfere with, impede, or object to the practice of the Catholic religion by the Catholic party and offspring; 2— the non-Catholic party does not impede the baptism and education of any of the offspring in the Catholic religion; and 3— the Catholic party strives prudently to effect the conversion of the non-Catholic spouse. This prudent effort implies that the Catholic party by the exemplary practice of his Faith will impress his conviction in that Faith upon the non-Catholic, and that his efforts at conversion are such that by their very nature they tend to ameliorate rather than alienate the non-Catholic's feelings toward the Catholic religion. If these conditions are had, not only will the *periculum* to the Faith of the Catholic consort become remote, but there also may be had a *spes conversionis* of the non-Catholic party. The presence of these precautions certainly is in keeping with the mind of the Church on this matter as expressed in an instruction of the Holy Office.[61]

The *periculum* mentioned in canon 1060, then, which is the reason for the prohibition of mixed marriages by the divine law, dictates the Church's effort to make certain that the religious Faith of the Catholic the essence of just what the *periculum* referred to in canon 1060 is, and in so doing leaves no doubt as to why this *periculum* must be avoided by Catholics. As long as the threat to the Faith is present, the prohibition of the divine law is present also. This fact necessitates the *cautiones* or guarantees treated above, and explains why the Church cannot dispense in any such case unless there is moral certitude concerning the fulfilling of these guarantees.

liberorum, et persaepe animos impellunt, ut cunctarum religionum aequam habere rationem assuescant, sublato veri falsique discrimine."—*Fontes,* n. 580.

[61] June 3, 1871—*Fontes,* n. 1013.

party will be protected from any and all probability of perversion before a dispensation from mixed religion or disparity of cult is granted.

In conclusion, the Church can and does sanate marriages contracted before a civil official or a non-Catholic minister invalidly under the accompaniment of the impediments either of disparity of cult or of mixed religion. The Church can do so if the source of the invalidity is founded only in a purely ecclesiastical law. However, since the conditions in either of these cases may actually entail also a prohibition of the divine law, as was explained above, the Church takes special precautions to remove the *periculum* mentioned in canon 1060, in order to safeguard and insure the Faith of the Catholic party and the offspring before granting a *sanatio in radice.*

CHAPTER IV

THIRD JURIDICAL EFFECT: DISPENSATION FROM THE LAW OF THE RENEWAL OF CONSENT

The third juridic effect of the *sanatio in radice* is a dispensation in the true meaning of the term. This effect is a relaxation of the law by which the Church demands a new exchange of consent by the parties before a convalidation can be confected.[1]

According to the wording of cannon 1138, § 1, the dispensation from the law of the renewal of consent is the third juridical effect contained in a radical sanation. However, in the logical order the dispensation from the law of the renewal of consent is the second effect, thus following immediately upon the dispensation from the impediment, if there be any, which obstructs the validity of marriage.[2] Once the impediment causing the invalidity of the marriage has been removed, the two parties are capable of exchanging a juridically efficacious consent that thus results in the convalidation of the marriage.

The writer does not intend to make a thorough investigation regarding the matter of marital consent, since that lies beyond the scope of this study. It is the purpose of the writer to treat in this chapter the dispensation from the law requiring the renewal of consent. In so doing he will consider in general: 1) the kind of consent required for a radical sanation; 2) the nature of defect of form marriages; 3) the question of the presence of consent when a given marriage already involves separation, divorce or a decree of nullity; 4) the time at which the dispensation takes effect, and 5) the effectiveness of the dispensation when the parties are opposed to receiving it.

For a deeper insight into the question of marital consent, other works treating precisely of this topic should be consulted.[3]

---

[1] Canons 1133-1135.

[2] *Supra*, p. 38.

[3] V.g., Courtemanche, *The Total Simulation of Matrimonial Consent*, The Catholic University of America Canon Law Studies, n. 270 (Washington, D.C.; The Catholic University of America Press, 1948); Griese, *The Marriage Contract and the Procreation of Offspring*, The Catholic University of America Canon Law Studies, n. 226 (Washington, D.C.; The Catholic University of

Article I. General Notions Concerning the Nature of the Consent Required

The very essence of marriage is the mutual exchange of consent by the parties contracting matrimony, and no human power is able to supply this consent.[4] Canon 1081, §2, defines matrimonial consent as "an act of the will by which each party gives and accepts the perpetual and exclusive right over the body, for acts which are of themselves suited for the generation of children." It is this consent as defined which must be present when a radical sanation is granted. The presence of this consent is a necessity demanded by the juridic effect discussed in this chapter, for how possibly could a convalidation containing a dispensation from the renewal of consent be effected if the required consent, the essence of marriage itself, were not actually in existence?

The essential importance of the matrimonial consent and the manner in which the *sanatio in radice* depends upon its presence is verified by canon 1139, §1, and canon 1140, §1 and §2. In these instances the entire strength of the canons hinges upon the matrimonial consent. This dependence is demonstrated by the use of the words *dummodo* and *si*. The use of these words together with the words *potest* and *nequit*[5] clearly emphasizes the fact enunciated in canon 1081, namely that the needed matrimonial consent cannot be supplied by any human authority or made up for by the ecclesiastical law. The legislator is incapable of subjecting the existence and the essence of the matrimonial consent to his law. Hence in these canons the legislator can do no

---

America Press, 1946); Timlin, *Conditional Matrimonial Consent*, The Catholic University of America Canon Law Studies, n. 89 (Washington, D.C.; The Catholic University of America Press, 1934); Dillon, *Common Law Marriages*, The Catholic University of America Canon Law Studies, n. 153 (Washington, D.C.; The Catholic University of America Press, 1942).

[4] Canon 1081, §1.

[5] Canon 1139, §1.—Quodlibet matrimonium initum cum utriusque partis consensu naturaliter sufficiente, sed iuridice inefficaci ob dirimens impedimentum juris ecclesiastici vel ob defectum legitimae formae, *potest* in radice sanari, *dummodo* consensus perseveret. Canon 1140, §1.—*Si* in utraque vel alterultra parte deficiat consensus, matrimonium *nequit* sanari in radice. §2. Quod *si* consensus ab initio quidem refuerit, sed postea praestitus fuerit, sanatio concedi *potest* a momento praestiti consensus.

more than rule that such a marriage can be sanated *in radice as long as* the consent perseveres, or that such a marriage cannot be sanated *if* the consent is lacking. The validity of the effects mentioned in these canons is essentially conditioned upon the presence of the matrimonial consent. This result affirms the transcendency of the consent as such beyond the scope of the legislator's power.

The exchange of consent upon which the granting of the radical sanation depends must be a true matrimonial, naturally valid (though juridically inefficacious) consent. That is to say, the two parties must have accepted each other as man and wife, with the intent and purpose of giving and receiving the rights over their bodies, and thus with the intention of entering marriage. However, juridically and in reality the exchange of such a consent results in but an imitation of marriage. This naturally valid exchange of marital consent is the *radix,* or root, that is fatally diseased by reason of its juridical inefficaciousness or invalidity. It is upon this *radix* that the extraordinary mode of convalidation, the *sanatio in radice,* reacts, sanating or healing the root by giving health or validity to what previously had only been an imitation of marriage.[6]

The naturally sufficient exchange of consent need not have been effected through an observance of the canonical form, for such an exchange of consent may be verified in a civil marriage so called, or in an attempted marriage before a non-Catholic minister. The truth of this statement is obvious from canon 1139, §1, which expressly adverts to the defect of legitimate form, and from the explicit mention in the Diocesan Quinquennial Faculties of marriages attempted before a civil official or a non-Catholic minister.[7] This fact is of great importance. For prior to the Code the question whether a union represented a *figura matrimonii* or a mere imitation of marriage meant a great deal in regard to radical sanation.

In this connection one needs to know the distinction between a *figura matrimonii* (semblance of marriage) and an imitation of marriage. By a *figura matrimonii* is meant an invalid marriage that nevertheless consists in the expression of marital consent according to the necessary

[6] Harrigan, pp. 2-3.

[7] "*Sanandi in radice matrimonia attentata coram officiali civili vel ministro acatholico.*" Cf. *supra,* p. 70.

substantial form.[8] By an imitation of marriage is meant an exchange of marital consent by the parties validly made in line with the requisites of the natural law, but invalid according to the law of the Church. Such an exchange of natural marital consent may be made in a civil ceremony, a non-Catholic religious ceremony, in a "common law" marriage without any ceremony, or it may be supplied during the course of the union if it was wanting at the time when the initial union was entered into.

After the *Tametsi* decree the *figura matrimonii* consisted in the observance of the canonical form prescribed by the Council of Trent.[9] During at least some period of time prior to the Code this *figura matrimonii* was, as a rule, a requisite in order that an invalid marriage could become the object of a radical sanation.[10] Pope Benedict XIV enforced this requirement,[11] and he refused to recognize any union devoid of the *figura matrimonii* as anything but a union involving fornication. This view of Pope Benedict XIV is quite evident in his prolific writings, especially in his letter *Redditae Nobis* of December 5, 1744, and his *De Synodo Dioecesana* of 1748.[12] Despite the staunch stand taken by Benedict XIV and other pontiffs[13] in the matter of not recognizing marriages lacking the *figura matrimonii* as anything but civil unions involving fornication, exceptions were made to the general rule that demanded this *figura matrimonii* as a requisite for the granting of a radical sanation. Examples of these exceptions prove that even prior to the Code sanations were granted, provided that a natural matrimonial consent was present.[14]

---

[8] Gallagher, *The Matrimonial Impediment of Public Propriety*, The Catholic University of America Canon Law Studies, n. 304 (Washington, D.C.; The Catholic University of America Press, 1952), p. 66; Gasparri, *De Matrimonio*, n. 47; Payen, *De Matrimonio in Missionibus*, I, n. 137.

[9] Conc. Trident., sess. XXIV, *de ref. matrim*, c. 1—Schroeder, *Canons and Decrees of the Council of Trent*, p. 184; Harrigan, p. 40.

[10] Gasparri, *De Matrimonio*, II, p. 1225; Cappello, *de Sacramentis*, V. De *Matrimonio*, n. 853; Harrigan, pp. 39-40.

[11] Harrigan, p. 40.

[12] Fontes n. 350; *De Synodo Dioecesana*, Lib. XIII, c. XXIV, n. 7.

[13] Benedictus XIV, litt. ap. *Exposuistis Nobis*, 17 Sept. 1746—*Collect, S. C. de Prop. Fide*, n. 359; Pius VI, *Perlatae sunt*, 28 maii 1793; Pius IX, allocut. *Acerbissimum*, 27 Sept. 1852—*Fontes* n. 515.

[14] S.C.S. Officii, 11 Nov. 1868—*Fontes*, n. 1004; 12 Apr. 1889—*Fontes* n. 1219.

What had been the exception to the rule in regard to the practice of the Church in sanating such invalid marriages (i.e., unions wanting the *figura matrimonii*) during the period from the Council of Trent to the promulgation of the Code became the ordinary practice of the Church with the introduction of the *Codex Iuris Canonici*. A putative marriage or the *figura matrimonii* no longer is required as the *radix* which is to be healed by a radical sanation. The text of canon 1139, §1, clearly indicates that a union evincing a true and naturally sufficient marital consent may be the object of a *sanatio in radice;* the *figura matrimonii* is not postulated in the present law as a necessity.[15]

When the parties have entered into a merely juridically inefficacious matrimonial union, the presumption of law favors the perseverance of consent, even though there may be knowledge of the nullity of the marriage, or even if the marriage be invalid because of the presence of an impediment, unless of course it is known that the consent has been revoked.[16]

The words *matrimonium* and *impedimenti* in canon 1093 do not refer only to marriages contracted according to the canonical form but invalid because of an impediment in the strict sense of the term. Rather, this canon includes also such unions as lack the required form as long as a true marital consent was exchanged. Marriages invalid by defect of form are designated with the word *matrimonium,* and the notion of defect of form can itself fall under the *notio impedimenti.* Thus the presumption of law according to the present mind of the Church favors these marriages, whereas prior to the Code the presumption favored only unions having the *figura matrimonii.*[17]

When treating the presumption of law mentioned in canon 1093, Payen stated that this presumption applies to marriages invalid by reason of an impediment of either the divine or the ecclesiastical law,

---

[15] Gasparri, *De Matrimonio,* II, n. 1225; Cappello, *De Sacramentis V De Matrimonio,* n. 853; Harrigan, pp. 40-41; Wernz-Vidal, *Ius Matrimoniale,* n. 665.

[16] Canon 1085—Scientia aut opinio nullitatis matrimonii consensum matrimonialem necessario non excludit.

Canon 1093—Etsi matrimonium invalide ratione impedimenti initum fuerit, consensus praestitus praesumitur perseverare, donec de eius revocatione constiterit.

[17] Cf. *supra,* p. 80.

whether the impediment be known or not, and also to marriages that lack all canonical form.[18] The presumption stands, he said, until the revocation of consent is established. Although one must make a prudent investigation in order to ascertain whether the consent perseveres, certitude is not required. Thus in a radical sanation the non-establishment of the revocation of consent suffices for a presumption of law favoring the perseverance of consent.[10] Prior to the Code the Church looked to the parties contracting the marriage, so that the presumption of law regarding the perseverance of consent depended upon the parties themselves. According to this manner of procedure a true marital consent was not to be presumed as present and persevering in parties who did not observe the canonical form, or who were incapacitated (*inhabiles*) because of an impediment. The presumption was rather that the consent given by these parties carried simply an intent of fornication. Today the Church looks to the consent itself rather than to the parties, and thus the presumption depends upon the effected exchange of consent. Persons expressing marital consent are presumed by canon 1086 to have the internal act of the will in conformity with their external manifestation. The fact that these parties enter a union devoid of canonical form, or invalid by reason of an impediment, does not destroy the presumption of the presence of a true marital consent and the latter perseverance of this consent. The Church looks directly to the consent itself in the forming of the presumption, so that the absence of juridically essential requisites (freedom from impediments, observance of the canonical form) does not affect this presumption.[19]

Therefore, ordinarily when parties seek a sanation, the natural consent is to be presumed as still persevering unless it is known that the consent has been revoked. If possible, a prudent investigation must be made concerning the perseverance of the consent.[20] The failure of such an investigation to disclose the revocation of the previously given consent allows a presumption in favor of the perseverance of the consent (canon 1093). A non-marital consent that signalizes simply an intent of fornication is obviously not an adequate consent in considera-

18 Harrigan, p. 88.

19 *De Matrimonio in Missionibus*, II, nn. 1748-1750.

19 Payen, *op cit.*, II, n. 1757.

20 Cf. can. 1139, §1, and can. 39.

tion of which a sanation could be granted. Parties who employ a civil ceremony, but who withhold marital consent with a view to observing the canonical form in the future, and to giving a true marital consent only at that time, cannot obtain a radical sanation of such an undertaking, whatever it may have been, for the reason simply that the exchange of a naturally sufficient consent was wanting at the time of the civil ceremony.

Parties living in concubinage cannot receive a radical sanation. Despite the semblance of conjugal life that usually accompanies concubinage, there is lacking the true marital consent that is postuated for a radical sanation.[21]

In many territories "common law" marriages are recognized by the states as valid marriages.[22] In these instances, if a true marital consent is exchanged, a "common law" marriage could very well be the object of a sanatio in radice.[23] The Code demands a true and naturally sufficient marital consent, but it does not demand that this consent be exchanged in a civil or religious ceremony. From the text of the Code there seems to be no basis for excluding "common law" marriages from the types of invalid unions that can be sanated. However, in practice it is to be doubted that a "common law" marriage would very often be the object of a sanation. There is such a close resemblance between it and concubinage, that it would be very difficult to ascertain whether or not true marital consent has been exchanged when the union was initiated, and whether it perseveres.[24] The absence of a public exchange of consent, such as is had in a non-Catholic religious ceremony or in a civil ceremony, would militate against the application of canon 1086, §1, and also in practice would hinder the including of such unions under the rule expressed in canon 1093.

The third juridic effect of a *sanatio in radice* may be said to be efficacious, provided that the recipients have the type of consent that

[21] Concubinage according to the mind of the Council of Trent was defined as a continued extra-marital sexual union between a man and a woman, regardless of the condition of either as a married or a single person. Cf. Gallagher, *The Matrimonial Impediment of Public Propriety*, p. 107.

[22] Dillon, *Common Law Marriages*, pp. 10-11.

[23] Dillon, *op. cit.*, pp. 85-86.

[24] Gallagher, *The Matrimonial Impediment of Public Propriety*, p. 102 ff.; Harrigan, p. 84.

is required by the Code. This consent must be a true marital consent which is sufficient according to the norms of the natural law. As long as this consent is had, it matters not whether the juridic ineffectiveness arose from the fact that the consent was exchanged in a non-Catholic religious ceremony, in a civil ceremony, or apart from any ceremony at all, or whether it arose through the presence of an impediment. Such is the effect and the application of canons 1139, §1, and 1140. Any type of consent which is not of a marital character definitely excludes the invalid marriage, if it can be called a marriage, from the reaping of any benefit by way of a radical sanation.

The dispensation from the renewal of consent that is contained in a radical sanation verifies the fact that a convalidation by this method is something positive. For by accepting the original or previous exchange of true marital consent, the Church is by ratification (*ratihabitio*) recognizing as a true marriage this presently continuing, naturally valid but heretofore juridically inefficacious contract.[25]

Article II. The Nature of Defect of Form Marriages

Earlier in this study[26] mention was made of the fact that one of the differences between simple convalidation and radical sanation is that in simple convalidation the canonical form is to be observed if it had been lacking, whereas in radical sanation the observance of the canonical form is dispensed with. Ordinarily when the prescribed canonical form[27] is lacking, the marriage in question is convalidated according to the norm of canon 1137.[28] However, if the conditions warrant it, a *sanatio in radice* can be invoked for the convalidating of a marriage invalid because of lack of canonical form.[29]

Two parties who are free from all diriment impediments can contract marriage invalidly in consequence of defect of form in various

---

[25] Cf. *supra,* p. 49.

[26] *Supra,* p. 44.

[27] Canon 1904.—Ea tantum matrimonia valida sunt quae contrahuntur coram parocho, vel loci Ordinario, vel sacerdote ab alterutro delegato et duobus saltem testibus, secundum tamen regulas expressas in canonibus qui sequuntur.

[28] "Matrimonium nullum of defectum formae, ut validum fiat, contrahi denuo debet legitima forma."

[29] Canon 1139, §1.

manners. The parties may attempt marriage before a civil magistrate or non-Catholic clergyman, thus contracting an invalid union. The parties may contract their marriage before a duly authorized priest but without the required witnesses, and in this case the marriage is also invalid. Finally, the parties may contract marriage in the presence of two witnesses but before a priest who lacks jurisdiction, and in this case the marriage also is invalid because of defect of canonical form. In any of these cases the marriages can be convalidated by way of a radical sanation, though a simple convalidation should be employed if that be at all feasible.

The Holy See has the power to sanate any marriage invalid in consequence of lack of canonical form, but the delegation of this power is made with restrictions. The faculty to sanate marriages invalid exclusively because of defect of form is not extended to ordinaries, but it is given to the Apostolic Delegate.[30] A restriction is placed upon the extension of the faculty to the Apostolic Delegate, inasmuch as he is not empowered to sanate a marriage invalid because of defect of form if neither of the parties involved are aware of the invalidity of the marriage.[31] If one of the parties is aware of the invalidity of the marriage, the Apostolic Delegate can sanate the marriage if he deems it deserving of this type of convalidation.

The fact that the Church places such restrictions upon the extending of the faculty to sanate marriages invalid because of defect of form seems to indicate its desire that all possible efforts be made for the convalidation of such marriages by means of a simple convalidation.

Article III. Question of the Perseverance of the Consent

Although parties involved in invalid marriages presumably have a true marital consent,[32] at times extraordinary circumstances apparently destroy this presumption. This apparent destruction of the perseverance gives rise to the question whether or not the invalid union involved is a fit object of a radical sanation. Separation from bed, board and cohabitation, divorce and a decree of nullity are circumstances that

[30] Harrigan, p. 147.

[31] Harrigan, p. 149.

[32] Cf. *supra*, p. 81 ff.

seemingly indicate a revocation of consent. Such a revocation naturally would remove the union in question from the orbit of radical sanation.

In separation from bed, board and cohabitation according to the norms of the Code[33] the parties, for just causes, disrupt their common life. This separation, be it permanent or temporary, could seemingly indicate a revocation of a marital consent. Generally such is not the case, however, for usually in a separation the parties quit their life in common but do not revoke their marital consent.[34] Theoretically an invalid union involving separation, despite the interruption or end of the common life, can be the object of a radical sanation. In practice however such an instance would be difficult to visualize. If the parties seeking the separation were aware of the invalidity of their union they would probably seek a decree of nullity thereby ending their mutual bonds. Upon consideration of the reasons that prompted the separation it seems unlikely, in view of their differences, that the parties would be content with a separation if a decree of nullity could be obtained. It is very improbable that the Church would sanate an invalid union if the parties actually are separated. If the parties have been reconciled when the sanation is petitioned for a perfect radical sanation is possible.[35] But in this case a thorough investigation of the status of the parties' consent during the period of separation should be made.

A civil divorce contains a stronger indication of the revocation of consent than does a separation. A civil divorce that is sought only for the civil effects as a complement to separation, or with the permission of the Church, would be considered in the same light as separation. However, a civil divorce that is sought as putting an end to marital life certainly has a different aspect than does a separation. By this type of divorce the parties (or at least one) indicate that they wish to sever all marital ties, thereby revoking their marital consent. Since the consent always had been juridically inefficacious, there is no change in the status of their union in the eyes of the Church. However, since the consent originally exchanged had been true marital, naturally sufficient consent, the divorce is tantamount to a destruction of that natural con-

[33] Canons 1128-1132.

[34] Wernz-Vidal, *Ius Matrimoniale,* n. 666, note 34, II; Harrigan, p. 90.

[35] Cf. preceding footnote.

sent. Obviously then no invalid union that ends in divorce would be presumed to have the marital consent still persevering.

In ascertaining whether or not marital consent is to be presumed to persevere in invalid marriages involving a petition for a degree of nullity, distinctions must be made. If one (or both) of the parties, when aware of the invalidity of the marriage seeks the decree of nullity, the logical conclusion is that the party wishes to terminate the union, and therefore revokes his consent.[86] However, if the party seeking the decree is uncertain of the invalidity of the marriage, then he is presumed to have revoked his consent provided the sentence is favorable to himself. Juridically then, the consent can be thought to persevere until after the sentence is rendered. If the sentence stands for the validity of the marriage and another impediment not indicated is discovered, a *sanatio in radice* could be granted.[87] Hence, in all such cases in respect to the perseverance of the consent, in practice a sufficient investigation must be made prior to the grant of a sanation in order to determine the actual status of the marital consent.

If a party other than the two joined in the union attacks thé validity of the marriage while the parties themselves stand for its validity, then consent is presumed to persevere. In this case if the marriage were declared null, then, since the parties indicated their continued marital consent by their stand, a radical sanation could be granted.[88]

A question of similar import is the following: What effect does a supervenient diriment impediment of the natural law have upon a true marital, though juridically inefficacious consent? The following case will illustrate the problem; John and Mary exchange a true marital consent that is juridically inefficacious because of a lack of canonical form. This marital consent perseveres, and the then, some period after the initial exchange of this consent, John becomes perpetually impotent.

---

[86] Gasparri, *De Matrimonio,* II, n. 1223; Wernz-Vidal, *Ius Matrimoniale,* n. 666, note 34, VI; Harrigan, p. 90.

[87] Gasparri, *loc. cit.;* Wernz-Vidal, *loc. cit.;* Harrigan, *loc. cit.* However, whether or not in a given case it would be advisable or even proper to grant a sanation may well depend on whether or not the other party is cognizant of this newly discovered impediment.—Cf. the case treated by Benedict XIV, Consti. *Cum super,* 25 Sept. 1755—*Bull. Rom. Cont.,* IV, 291; Cf. Wernz-Vidal, *Ius Matrimoniale,* n. 666, note 32; Harrigan, p. 92.

[88] Wernz-Vidal, *op. cit.,* n. 666, note 34 VII; Harrigan, p. 92.

The consent still continues, and then, after another interval of time, a *sanatio in radice* is sought. The question is, can a radical sanation be given for this union? Feije (1820-1894) claimed that a sanation could be granted because a radical sanation heals the consent at its very inception.[39] However, this position does not appear tenable. Other authors[40] are quick to reject Feije's view, and the reason is clear.

Despite the element of retroactivity contained in a *sanatio in radice*, the convalidation itself is effected *ex nunc* at the time when the favor is granted.[41] Now, at the very time when the favor could be granted, John is incapable of contracting marriage because of his impotence, and so a convalidation is impossible. The incurring of this impediment of the natural law vitiates the natural consent and renders it worthless. John cannot give the marital consent required by canon 1181, §2.[42] John is no longer capable of performing the conjugal act, and hence he cannot give the right to the performance of this act. No valid marriage can be contracted in view of this fact.[43] Therefore no radical sanation is possible in this case.

For unions in which there exists an impediment of the natural law (no matter when that impediment arose), an all-inclusive rule bars all such marriages from the possibility of being sanated. This rule obviously is founded on the inability of the Church to dispense from impediments of the natural law.[44] However, in regard to union wherein separation, divorce or a decree of nullity has intervened, individual attention must be given to each case. What seems indicated in general may not be true in a particular case, and thus it remains necessary to

---

39 Feije, *De Impedimentis et Dispensationibus Matrimonialibus*, n. 769.

40 Payen, *De matrimonio in Missionibus*, II, n. 2615; Wernz-Vidal, *Ius Matrimoniale*, n. 663, note 25; Harrigan, p. 94.

41 Cf. *supra*, p. 48 ff.

42 "Consensus matrimonialis est actus voluntatis quo utraque pars tradit et acceptat ius in corpus, perpetuum et exclusivum, in ordine ad actus pro se aptos ad prolis generationem."

43 Can. 1086, §2, si . . . excludat . . . omne ius ad conjugalem actum. . . . invalide contrahit. Cf. can. 1015, §1, 1111; McCarthy, *The Matrimonial Impediment of Impotence with Special Reference to the Physical Capacity for Marriage of an "Excised Woman" and of a "Doubly Vasectomised" Man*, (Romae: Catholic Book Agency, 1948), pp. 26 ff. Cappello, De Sacramentis, V, *De Matrimonio*, n. 347.

44 Cf. *supra*, pp. 51 ff.

make an investigation regarding the perseverance of the consent in the parties. This individual attention one must give in order to be able to ascertain whether a true marital consent is present and has persevered, and whether a radical sanation can be granted in this instance.

Article IV. Time at Which the Dispensation from the Renewal of Consent Takes Effect

In regard to the time element involved in granting the dispensation from the law of the renewal of consent, there is to be considered, the point of time at which this dispensation takes effect. The point of time at which the mutual, abiding consent, which is presently to be sanated, came into being does not concern this question. The initial point of this mutual, abiding consent is the *radix* of the invalid union and has respect only to the canonical effects which are the fourth and logically the last result of the *sanatio in radice.* This matter, therefore, will be treated in dealing with the canonical effects of radical sanation.

The point of time at which the dispensation from the law of the renewal of consent takes effect is rather evident and presents no problem whatsoever. Similar to the convalidation of the marriage itself, (which latter effect of sanation is immediately preceded by the dispensation from renewal of consent in the logical order), the dispensation from the renewal of consent takes effect *ex nunc,* or as of the time when the radical sanation is granted.[45] If the law requiring the renewal of consent were enforced, then the consent would be exchanged at the time when the convalidation is being effected, or *ex nunc.* Hence it necessarily follows that the dispensation from the law of the renewal of consent takes effect *ex nunc,* or as of the time when under ordinary circumstances, i.e., in a simple convalidation the consent would be renewed.

Article V. Effectiveness of the Grant of Sanation for Unwilling Parties

A problem that centers chiefly around the dispensation from the renewal of consent is the following one. Can a *sanatio in radice* be granted if both parties are opposed to the convalidation of the invalid

[45] Cf. *Supra,* p. 86 ff.

union. The problem has its practical value in the granting of general sanations. The unwillingness of the parties to have their union convalidated may be indicated by the refusal of the parties to renew their marital consent before the Church or before witnesses.

Cappello holds that the Roman Pontiff can most certainly sanate invalid unions even though both spouses are unwilling to receive the radical sanation. This grant presumes, of course, that the required conditions for the granting of a radical sanation are present. Cappello adds, however, that *de facto* the Holy Father does not follow the practice of granting such a sanation in particular cases. In the case of a sanation, improperly so called, wherein only the canonical effects of the union, and not the convalidation, are granted, a radical sanation would more readily be conceded over the opposition of the parties. In regard to general sanation, Cappello says that all unions falling within the scope of the grant are sanated as long as a true marital consent perseveres. Whether the parties are willing or not, and whether they know it or not, their invalid marriages are convalidated and therefore are valid in the eyes of the Church.[46] Vromant appears to be of much the same mind as Cappello in this matter, and his opinion seems to be substantially similar to it.[47]

Payen took the opposite view. He held that if both parties are unwilling to receive a *sanatio in radice,* then it cannot be given. For his reason Payen pointed to the unworthiness of the parties. He claimed that the contempt for the ecclesiastical law by the parties made them unworhy of such a favor from the Church.[48] Payen cited Noldin, who likewise held that if both parties opposed the radical sanation it could not be given. Contumacy with reference to the laws of the Church was given as the reason by Noldin. He stands that in view of this contumacy it was only prayers for the eternal salvation of their souls that could be invoked for the parties. Noldin tempered his view somewhat, however, by adding that, if the parties oppose the *sanatio in*

---

[46] *De Sacramentis,* V, *De Matrimonio,* n. 852, §4.

[47] Vromant, Ius Missionariorum (6 vols., Vol. V, *De Matrimonio,* Louvanii: Museum Lessianum, 1931), n. 251.

[48] *De Matrimonio in Missionibus,* II, n. 2617, §2.

radice for a grave reason, then the contumacy disappears and a radical sanation becomes possible.[49]

The Code itself does not treat this problem directly. In canon 1138, §3, the Code states definitely that a dispensation from the renewal of consent can be given if one, or both, parties are unaware of the grant.[50] The Code does not mention anything specifically in regard to the unwillingess of the parties to receive a radical sanation. A case of the following type would appear to be what the legislator had in mind as the object of canon 1138, §3: John and Mary neither bound by a diriment impediment contract marriage before the Church. However, unbeknown to the parties, the priest who assists at the ceremony lacks authorization. Once this condition is discovered, the priest rather than cause grave trouble of soul for parties by informing them of the situation, petitions for a *sanatio in radice.* The radical sanation is granted, and the parties are never made aware of the grant or of the real juridic state of their earlier putative marriage. In this case there is no knowledge on the part of the consorts, but neither is there any unwillingness. In fact, if the truth were known by them, the parties very probably would have desired the sanation.

Quite often one party may be opposed to receiving the sanation. This situation may occur when the non-Catholic party refuses to renew consent before the Church. The basis of the refusal more often than not is that the non-Catholic considers the attempted marriage as valid, and he does not wish to have the Church convalidate the marriage, since that could show his acceptance of the Church's jurisdiction over his marriage. It would also be tantamount to an admission by him that he was living in an invalid marriage. However, despite this opposition to the convalidation the marital consent and other requisites for a radical sanation are present. Hence a *sanatio in radice* will be granted over the opposition of the non-Catholic and without his knowledge in order to spiritually benefit the Catholic party and the offspring. A very different case is presented however, if the Catholic as well as the non-Catholic party refuses to renew consent before the Church. Both parties appear to oppose the convalidation. Noldin had such a case in mind

[49] *Summa Theologiae Moralis,* III, n. 660.

[50] "Dispensatio a lege de renovando consensu concedi etiam potest vel una vel utraque parte inscia."

when he said that owing to the contumacy of the parties no sanation could be given.[51] This also appears to be the reason why Capello and Vromant hold that *de facto* the Church would not be wont to grant a radical sanation in a particular case to parties possessing such an attitude.[52] In an individual instance, then the question is more or less theoretical. However, in the case of a general sanation, the question becomes more practical. The question is whether an individual invalid marriage wherein both parties oppose a convalidation is convalidated if a general sanation has been granted in a locality.

It appears to the writer that the view of Cappello and Vromant is preferable to that of Payen. The *sanatio in radice,* being an extraordinary favor, depends upon the benign will of the Church. Certainly, the will of the Church takes precedence over the will of the parties. If the Church desires to grant this favor, and the requisites for its validity are present, the opposition of the parties would not seem to be sufficient to withstand this desire; otherwise it would seem that the subjects of the law were overruling the legislator.

Payen's view gives rise to difficulties in regard to general sanations. If his view were correct then when a general sanation is granted all, a great many, a few, or perhaps even no invalid marriages may admit of convalidation. In practice it would be exceedingly difficult to ascertain which unions remained invalid. This view also would open the door to unscrupulous persons if they later wished to attempt another marriage. These persons could claim that their previous union was not sanated owing to their unwillingness, and now they desire to contract another marriage before the Church.

The problem is one that does not admit of a facile solution. Harrigan does not concern himself seriously with the problem as he assumes that the sanation can be granted whether the parties be willing or not. He states that canon 37 obviates whatever difficulty may derive through canon 1138, §3.[53] This canon states that a rescript may be gained for one without his consent and that the favor is valid before its acceptance.

---

[51] *Summa Theologiae Moralis,* III, n. 660.

[52] Capello De Sacramentis, V, *De Matrimonio,* n. 852, §4; Vromant, *De Matrimonio,* n. 251.

[53] Harrigan, pp. 77-78.

The writer thinks that the problem cannot be dismissed that easily. In regard to baptized persons the following general rule would seem to apply: whether the parties opposed the sanation or not their marriage would be convalidated, provided of course that on their part a true marital consent persevered. This conclusion logically follows from the invalidity of the union (and also dispenses from the renewing of the consent), then the baptized parties cannot have true marital consent without receiving the sacrament of matrimony.[54] The parties cannot divorce their marital consent from the sacramental contract. Therefore the parties cannot possess a true marital consent and yet remain in an invalid union after the general sanation. Either they receive the sacrament and have their marriage convalidated, or else their consent is merely fornicarious.

The unwillingness of the parties to receive a sanation certainly calls for an investigation if one is to determine whether or not a true marital consent still perseveres. If both parties opposed the convalidation of their marriage by way of a radical sanation such opposition from them appears to destroy the presumption favoring the perseverance of their marital consent. The facts seem to indicate the presence of nothing more than a permanent desire for a life of fornication.

The writer believes that the following conclusion may be safely adopted: The Church can grant a radical sanation, even though both parties are opposed to it, provided always that their originally exchanged marital consent perseveres in the present. However, an investigation must be made in each case if one is reliably to determine whether or not the unwillingness entails also the non-perserverance of a true marital consent on their part. If it does, then obviously no radical sanation can be effected.

---

[54]Canon 1012, §2. "Quare inter baptizatos nequit matrominialis contractus validus consistere, quin sit eo ipso sacramentum."

CHAPTER V

FOURTH JURIDICAL EFFECT: RETROACTION OF THE CANONICAL EFFECTS TO THE PAST

Article I. Preliminary Notions

The fourth juridic effect of a radical sanation according to both the logical order[1] and the order in the Code[2] is the bestowal of the canonical effects retroactively, through a fiction of the law, to the past.[3] This fourth effect is the legitimation, in regard to all canonical effects, of the offspring produced in the sanated marriage during the period of its juridically inefficacious existence.[4] The placing of this effect in the fourth and last place of the logical sequence of the four favors contained in a radical sanation is obvious. The canonical effects are but a natural result produced, once the union is convalidated. The effects cannot precede the cause.

Harrigan states that the canonical effects of marriage are set forth in canons 1110 to 1117 inclusively.[5] This statement cannot be accepted only with a modification that is in keeping with the provisions of each of these canons respectively. Harrigan confuses the effects of marriage as such with the canonical effects of matrimony. His position leads to conclusions that cannot possibly be sustained or accepted. Following his statement to its logical conclusion, one would necessarily have to hold that the sacramental grace conferred by the sacrament of matrimony[6] is granted retroactively to the parties. Thus it would be effective at the inception of the invalid marriage. This conclusion obviously is theologically impossible. Since the convalidation is effective *ex nunc*, the sacrament itself is received *ex nunc*, and hence the sacra-

---

[1] Cf. *supra*, p. 38.

[2] Canon 1138, §1.

[3] Canon 1138, §1.—" . . . retroactionem, per fictionem iuris, circa effectus canonicos, ad praeteritum."

[4] Gasparri, *De Matrimonio*, II, n. 1213; Wernz-Vidal, *Ius Matrimoniale*, n. 658; Cappelo, *De Sacramentis*, V, *De Matrimonio*, n. 857; Payen, *De Matrimonio in Missionibus*, II, n. 2600.

[5] *The Radical Sanation of Invalid Marriages*, p. 49.

[6] Canon 1110.

mental grace also. Under no circumstances could sacramental grace be construed as being conferred apart from a sacrament being conferred also. Harrigan's statement would also mean that the conjugal rights[7] would be granted to the parties retroactively. The metaphysical impossibility of such an event has already been discussed.[8] Harrigan himself at another point in his work condemns such a view.[9]

The fourth effect of a radical sanation then is the legitimation of the offspring, retroactive to the inception of the *radix* sanated, in regard to all of its canonical incidents. These canonical effects are not to be confused with the marital effects that are proper to the parties themselves, and which are operative *ex nunc,* at the time of the grant of the *sanatio in radice.*

Of the four favors contained in a radical sanation the element of retroactivity reveals the most extraordinary quality. As has been stated in preceding chapters, the element of retroaction refers only to the bestowal of the canonical effects. There is no retroaction in regard to the convalidation of the marriage, to the dispensation from the inpediment (if there be any), or to the dispensation from the renewal of consent. These first three juridic effects of a radical sanation become effective at the moment the grant is made, or *ex nunc.* Since the marriage is convalidated *ex nunc* the dispensation from the impediment and the dispensation from the law of the renewal of consent are required *ex nunc* also. There appears to be no reason why two latter dispensations should be fictitiously granted *ex tunc,* since the convalidation for which they are requisites is not to be construed as having been granted *ex tunc.*[10]

In the chapter regarding the convalidation of the marriage the wording of canon 1138, §1, was used as an argument to demonstrate that the convalidation is not to be thought of as having been granted *ex tunc.*[11] This same argument applies here to indicate that, in addition to the convalidation, the legislator also had in mind the dispensation from the impediment and the dispensation from the law of the renewal of con-

---

7 Canon 1111.

8 Cf. supra, p. 23.

9 *Op. cit.,* pp. 45-46.

10 Cf. supra, p. 50 ff.

11 Cf. *supra,* p. 52.

sent as occurring *ex nunc,* and not *ex tunc through* a fiction of law. The placing of the phrase, "*et retrotractionem, per fictionem iuris,* directly before "*circa effectus canonicos, ad praeteritum*" is indicative to the writer that the retroaction refers to the canonical effects of the marriage and to these canonical effects alone.

Harrigan states in his study that the effects of radical sanation are essentially two: the convalidation of the marriage and the legitimation of any children born of the previously invalid marriage.[12] Earlier in this work the writer listed the juridic effects of a *sanatio in radice* as four, in line with the text of canon 1138, §1. It is according to this latter listing that this work is divided.[13] However, since the dispensation from the impediment and the dispensation from the law of the renewal of consent are usually considered in connection with the convalidation of the marriage, Harrigan's statement is quite acceptable.

In addition to Harrigan's statement concerning the division of the effects of radical sanation, it may be further stated that the juridic effects (since they are favors[14]) allow of a division that looks to the beneficiaries of the radical sanation. The first juridic effect, the convalidation of the marriage, is a benefit for the spouses whose marriage was convalidated. The second juridic effect, that of legitimation, is a benefit for the offspring, which otherwise, in consequence of the fault of the parents, would be laboring under the stigma of illegitimacy. It seems only fitting that the offspring which, through no fault of its own has incurred this juridic disability should benefit from the retroactive element contained in convalidation by radical sanation.

The remainder of this chapter will deal with the point of time in respect to the *radix* to which the retroaction reaches, the manner in which the retroaction is effected, legitimation in its fundamental concept, and the specific applicability of the legitimation granted in a radical sanation.

Article II. The *Radix*

Canon 1138, §1, is not very explicit in determining to just what

---

[12] *Op. cit.,* p. 43.

[13] Cf. supra, p. 37.

[14] Cf. *supra,* p. 37.

point in time the retroaction of the canonical effects reverts. The canon merely states, *ad praeteritum,* to the past. However, the apparent vagueness of canon 1138, §1, in this matter is cleared considerably by canon 1138, §2, and canon 1140, §2.[15] This point of origin (as well as of the continuation of the consent) whence the canonical effects become operative after the grant of a sanation is termed the *radix* of the marriage. This *radix* is that upon which a *sanatio in radice* acts.

Cappello gives an excellent definition of the *radix* of the invalid marriage. He states that the *radix,* in which the marriage is said to be sanated, is the consent, naturally efficacious, previously elicited and persevering up to the present.[16] By breaking down Cappello's definition and examining it more carefully, one may note more clearly all of the elements that constitute the *radix.*

1. *Radix, in qua coniugium dicitur sanari*—The root is the element upon which the radical sanation acts. In other words, it is the root of the marriage diseased by invalidity. Since the root, or source, of the marriage is diseased, the remainder of the union will be diseased also. In order to heal this invalid union at its very source a *sanatio in radice* is granted.

2. *Est consensus*—The root in which the invalid marriage is healed is the marital consent itself. It is this exchange of consent that makes the marriage and is of the very essence of the marriage, and so it is this consent that must be acknowledged as the root or source of the marriage.[17]

3. *Naturaliter efficax*—The consent exchanged by the parties must be naturally efficacious. The two parties must truly exchange a marital consent, they must take each other as man and wife, they must give and receive the perpetual and exclusive right over their bodies for the act which inherently is suited for the generation of offspring.[18]

---

[15] Canon 1138, §2: Convalidatio fit a momento concessionis gratiae; retroactio vero intelligitur facta ad matrimonii initium, nisi aliud expresse caveatur.

Canon 1140, §2: Quod si consensus ab initio quidem defuerit, sed postea praestitus fuerit, sanatio concedi potest a momento praestiti consensus.

[16] *De Sacramentis,* V, *De Matrimonio,* n. 859, bis: "Radix, in qua coniugium dicitur sanari, est consensus, naturaliter efficax, praevie elicitus et adhuc perseverans."

[17] Canon 1081.

[18] Canon 1081.

The reason for the invalidity of the union must be sought, not in the consent itself, but rather in conditions attached to this marital consent by canonical legislation. It is the non-fulfilment of these conditions that renders the true marital consent juridically inefficacious.

4. *Praevie elicitus*—The consent is not exchanged *ex nunc,* or at the time when the radical sanation is granted, but has already been given. The exchange of a true marital consent at the beginning of the invalid union suffices, so that no new exchange of consent is required later in connection with the sanation itself.

5. *Adhuc perseverans*—The true marital consent once exchanged must have been revoked, but must be persevering at the time when the *sanatio in radice* is granted. If the consent is not persevering then, it is non-existent, and there is no marriage to convalidate or sanate. Although the *radix* is often spoken of as though it were only the initial point of the abiding naturally efficacious consent, it is in reality the entire uninterrupted continuance of the marital consent from its inception to the time of the radical sanation.

Since this naturally sufficient and subsequently abiding marital consent begins at different points in various unions, the *radix* or object of the radical sanation is a matter of variable fact. That is, the point of time at which there was exchanged the true marital consent that later becomes susceptible to sanation may well vary from one marriage to another. Thus no general, all-inclusive rule concerning this point of time may be made. Rather this fact must be ascertained in each particular case.[19]

In a perfect radical sanation the *radix* of the invalid marriage is the exchange of the true marital consent that was made when the union was first initiated, and which continues to the time of the sanation. This *radix* depends solely upon the natural efficaciousness of the exchange of the consent. The fact that this juridical inefficacious exchange of consent was made in a non-Catholic religious ceremony, in a civil ceremony, or apart from any ceremony at all, does not affect the *radix* in the least. In regard to all perfect sanations, there is no difficulty concerning the point of time at which the *radix* comes into being. The question is rather whether a perfect radical sanation is possible, in a given case.

[19] Cf. canons 1139, §1, and 1140.

The expression, "perfect" *sanatio in radice,* by force of its very definition postulates the initial exchange of a true, naturally sufficient, and subsequently abiding, marital consent at the very outset of the juridically inefficacious union.[20] If the root of the invalid marriage which awaits its sanation is to be sought at any point of time other than the moment the invalid marital union was first entered, then the radical sanation *ipso facto* cannot be a perfect radical sanation.

The *radix* in an imperfect radical sanation[21] is thus in fact a variable thing which may differ from case to case. According to the circumstances, the *radix* may be established shortly after the beginning of the invalid union, midway in the course of the union, or shortly before the *sanatio in radice* is sought. The reason for these contingencies is that one or both parties did not give a true marital consent when the invalid union was first entered, but later on in the course of the union supplied the required consent. In any such case the point of time at which the naturally required consent is supplied, if it then continues to abide to the time of the sanation, marks the *radix* of the union.[22]

Perrone proffered the view that, as long as a true, naturally sufficient, marital consent had been once exchanged, a radical sanation could be granted. The fact that this consent was later revoked and did not persevere at the time of the grant did not preclude the granting of a sanation according to this view. It was claimed that the radical sanation healed the marital consent at its inception, and hence this was the only point of time in the union that actually required the presence of the true marital consent.[23] This opinion cannot be held in the face of canon 1140, §1. No modern author accepts this opinion of Perrone, and it is untenable not only by reason of canon 1140, §1, but also because it implies that the sacrament of matrimony can be effected without the presence of marital consent.[24] For Perrone, then, no *radix* was

---

20 Cf. *supra,* p. 5.

21 E.g., a sanation imperfect in consequence of a previous substantial defect in the exchanged consent. Cf. canons 1082-1083; 1086, §2; 1087, §1; 1089, §3; 1092, §1, §2; and 1140.

22 Canon 1140, §2.

23 *De Matrimonio Christiano,* II, 173 ff.

24 Gasparri, *De Matrimonio,* II, n. 1222; Payen, *De Matrimonio in Missionibus,* II, n. 2615; Harrigan, p. 88; Capello, *De Sacramentis,* V, *De Matrimonio,* n. 853, §3.

required, since he did not demand that the consent persevere. This position, of course, is contrary to the very nature of a *sanatio in radice.*

There appears to be a problem as to just what constitutes the *radix* in a case of the following type: John and Mary exchange a true, naturally sufficient, marital consent at the beginning of their invalid union. Later on in the course of the union this consent is revoked. At a still later point of time the consent is once more given. A radical sanation is sought, and since the required consent is present the favor can be granted. In the case as outlined, where does the *radix* of the union begin? Does it originate at the first exchange of the true marital consent, or did the subsequent revocation destroy this root so that the real *radix* begins at the moment when a true marital consent is again supplied?

Canon 1140 does not deal precisely with a case of this nature. The canon states that, if consent is lacking at the inception of the union and then is supplied later, the union is sanated from the moment that the consent is supplied. The canon does not explicitly envision a case in which the true marital consent is given, then later on revoked, and once more exchanged, so that the required marital consent is present at the time of the radical sanation.[25]

Gasparri stated explicity that in a case of this type a complete sanation and one properly so called is possible.[26] Did Gasparri mean by *plena et proprie dicta* that the root of the union is the first exchange of a true marital consent at the inception of the invalid union? The fact that in the preceding paragraph Gasparri treated of the case envisioned by canon 1140, §2, illuminates his meaning somewhat. In this instance he stated that, if consent is lacking *ab initio* but later is given and is present when the sanation is sought, a *sanatio imperfecta et improprie dicta* is possible.[27] From a comparison of the use of terms in these two instances, it seems to the writer that Gasparri identified the point of time of the *radix* with the point of time of the first exchange

---

[25] Canon 1140, §2.—Quod si consensus ab initio quidem defuerit, sed postea praestitus fuerit, sanatio concedi potest a momento praestiti consensus.

[26] *De Matrimonio,* II, n. 1222: "Quod si consensus ab initio adfuit, deinde revocatus fuit, sed postea rursus positus, momento sanationis adest, sanatio in radice plena et proprie dicta possibilis est."

[27] *Op. cit.,* II, n. 1221.

of consent at the beginning of the invalid union. The subsequent interruption in the continuance of the consent could thus be regarded as not completely destroying the character of its fundamental perseverance, provided the consent was again supplied and was present at the time of the sanation.

Payen stated that in such a case at least an imperfect sanation is possible. However, he then added in a footnote that Gasparri held that a perfect sanation could be given.[28] Payen's definition of a perfect sanation runs as follows: a perfect sanation contains all those things which according to canon 1138, §1, §2, constitute a radical sanation. He then adds that one of the things that makes a sanation imperfect is the want of consent at the outset of the union, which want dictates the retroaction of the canonical effects to only that moment at which this want of consent was supplied.[29] Although Payen may have wished to agree with Gasparri in stating that a perfect sanation can be given in the case of a "restored" consent, he nevertheless preferred to restrict himself to saying that *at least* an imperfect sanation can be granted.[30]

Harrigan likewise stated that in this case a complete sanation can be given. Harrigan, however, did not treat the matter any further; he merely cited Gasparri, and seemed to assume that no particular difficulty or question was involved.[31]

Certainly if Gasparri meant by a full and proper sanation that the first exchange of consent constitutes the initial point of time of the *radix,* the opinion would carry considerable weight. As President of the Code Commission, and as having written his work *according to the mind of the Code,* he certainly could not be denied the possession of a great capacity for accurately interpreting the mind of the legislator. Despite this fact, however, the writer cannot accept the proposed view. Since the union in question is a juridically inefficacious union

---

[28] *De Matrimonio in Missionibus,* II, n. 2615, note 1: "C. Gasparri, II, n. 1222, censet, ut diximus (n. 2608, note 1), eo in casu, posee concedi sanationem perfectam."

[29] *Op. cit.,* II, n. 2608, 3°.

[30] *Op. cit.,* II, p. 907, note 1: After quoting Gasparri's opinion from the latter's work, n. 1222, Payen concluded: "Dicamus potius: Saltem concedi potest sanatio imperfecta (*infra,* n. 2615).

[31] *The Radical Sanation of Invalid Marriages,* p. 86.

it is not indissoluble.[32] No true marriage obtains, for the parties have not exchanged their marital consent according to the form demanded as essential by the laws of the Church. Since in this instance at least one of the parties is baptized, the union is subject to the ecclesiastical law.[33] In view of these facts it appears to the writer that any revocation of marital consent will destroy the marital aspect of that union. To hold that, after the revocation of this consent, a supplying of the consent will again restore the union in such a manner that the original marital consent can be considered as having persevered in its entirety seems opposed to canon 1081. If such a "constructive" perseverance were to be maintained, the Church would appear to be supplying the marital consent for the interim during which it remained revoked. Once an interruption has been made in the continuance of the consent, there is no human way to bridge this interval; a new *radix* must begin with the new exchange of a truly marital consent.

The *radix* then depends upon the exchange of a true marital consent and the uninterrupted perseverance of that consent. In a perfect radical sanation the *radix* extends from the moment when the invalid union was first entered until the time when the sanation is granted. In an imperfect radical sanation the *radix* begins at the moment when the defective consent was supplied, provided that this supplied consent persevered until the very moment of the granted sanation. This latter statement is true, even though there existed an earlier given consent which later was revoked. The retroaction of the canonical effects depends upon the inception of the *radix*. Through a fiction of the law these effects are granted retroactively to the moment when the *radix* itself gained actual existence.

Article III. The *Fictio Iuris*

There is nothing out of the ordinary in the granting of the canonical effects in connection with the convalidation of an invalid union. However, when the granting of these canonical effects is done in such a manner that they are bestowed retroactively, the grant is indeed extraordinary. Such is the case with the *sanatio in radice*. The canonical

---

[32] Canon 1013, §2; Wernz-Vidal, *Ius Matrimoniale*, n.n. 583 ff.

[33] Canon 87.

effects are granted retroactively to the past, to the beginning of the invalid union.[34]

It must be remembered that this retroactive grant depends upon a fiction of law. Canon 1138, §1, does not state that in reality the canonical effects are granted retroactively. The canon states that through a *fiction of law* the canonical effects are granted retroactively. That is to say, the canonical effects are considered as though they were present *ab initio* although in reality they came into being only at the moment of the grant.[35]

Prior to the Code the element of retroaction proved itself a serious problem for canonists treating the *sanatio in radice.* The pre-Code canonists attempted to explain the element of retroaction in various ways. Some authors explained it by stating that the union was convalidated *ex tunc.* This explanation facilitated the comprehending of the idea of retroaction, but, as discussed earlier, the view proposed a solution that was metaphysically impossible.[36] Another school of thought explained the element of retroaction in radical sanation in the following manner: The convalidation itself was effected *ex nunc,* but there was a retroactive abrogation of the canon law establishing this impediment. This abrogation opened the way for the flow of the canonical effects. Hence, even though the union was valid *ex nunc,* the canonical effects were produced *ex tunc.* This view was held by Benedict XIV.[37]

The element of retroaction in the Code is explained by the use of a precise juridic device termed a fiction of law. The fiction of law is not

---

[34] Canon 1138, §1; *supra,* art. II.

[35] Payen, *De Matrimonio in Missionibus,* II, n. 2600; Gasparri, *De Matrimonio,* II, n. 1209; Harrigan, p. 9.

[36] *Supra,* pp. 28-29; Gasparri, *De Matrimonio,* II, n. 1208; Harrigan, pp. 9-10.

[37] *Quaestiones Canonicae,* q. 174, §2: "Summus Pontifex potest legem ecclesiasticam irritare et revocare non tantum quoad imposterum secuturos effectus, no incurrantus, sed etiam quoad effectus antes productos iuxta textum in Clemintina quoniam, *de. imm. eccles.* sic dispensando in radice et revocando impedimentum dirimens matrimonium et simul et semel abrogando legem ecclesiasticam, quae dictum statuit impedimentum, facit ut dispensation retrobatur ad initium matrimonii et sic quod prolos quoad omnes effectus . . . legitima sit et habeatur."

a development of canon law; rather, it had its origin in Roman Law.[38] The accepted definition of a fiction of law is that given by Alciatus: the fiction of law "is a rule of law which assumes as true, for a just cause, something which is false but not impossible."[39] In Roman Law the *fictio iuris* could not be employed unless all of the conditions embodied in the definition were fulfilled. The fiction of law in canon law is substantially the same as the *fictio iuris* of Roman Law. Hence, there are conditions to be fulfilled before a radical sanation with its element of retroaction can be granted.

The purpose of the fiction of law in canon 1138, §1, is the granting of the canonical effects retroactively to the very beginning, the *radix,* of the invalid union. In accord with the nature of the fiction of law the retroaction of the canonical effects is produced in the following manner:

At the time when the radical sanation is sought, the canonical effects are non-existent because of the juridical inefficaciousness of the invalid union. These canonical effects, then are the element that is false, but by reason of the fiction of the law inherent in the grant of the sanation are assumed to be true.

There must be a just cause for the assumption. The just cause in this case is fulfilled by the sufficient reasons that prompt the granting of the convalidation by virtue of a radical sanation.

Although false (or non-existent), it must have been possible for the canonical effects truly to exist at the *terminus ad quem* of the retroaction. Since there is an invalid marital union existing in the past as the point of the retroaction, this condition is verified. Canonical effects can be produced by an invalid marriage.[40] Thus, even though the invalid union in a given case *de facto* does not produce the canonical effects of marriage, this occurrence is not impossible.

All of the required conditions of the *fictio iuris* are present in the fiction of law as it operates in regard to the retroaction of a radical sanation. The canonical effects are the object of the fiction of the law. These canonical effects are the false element that is assumed to be true.

---

[38] *Supra,* p. 29; Inst. 2(12.5): D. 28(1.12), 49(15.18).

[39] Cicognani, *Canon Law,* pp. 535-536; "Fictio enim est legis adversus veritatem in re possibili ex iusta causa dispositio."

[40] Cf. canon 1114; canonical effects are produced by a putative marriage which is in reality invalid.

The necessary conditions for the granting of the radical sanation constitute the just cause which is required for the fiction of law to become operative.[41] The fact that the terminal point of the retroaction is an invalid marital union entered into in the past makes the existence of the canonical effects a possibility at that point.

It is through this fiction of law then that the legitimation of the offspring is effected retroactively to the past. The *fictio iuris* is the vehicle that transports retroactively the canonical effects to a point of time in the past. The fact cannot be changed that the beneficiary of the fiction of the law was actually born illegitimate. "*Infectum fieri non potest factum.*" However, the offspring is considered as though he were born legitimate, and through this fiction of law he is entitled to the canonical effects that accompany legitimate birth.[42]

The manner of retroaction in canon 1138, §1, is produced by a fiction of law. It now remains to treat the result of this fiction (i.e., the legitimation of the offspring) and the specific applicability of the legitimation granted in a radical sanation.

Article IV. Legitimation in its Fundamental Concept

The result produced by the fiction of law in canon 1138, §1, is the retroactive legitimation of the offspring together with the canonical effects that accompany legitimacy.[43] Various authors have defined legitimation in various ways, but in substance these definitions are quite similar. The writer follows the example of McDevitt[44] and adopts the definition of legitimation as given by Vermeersch-Creusen: "Legitimation is a benefit of the law or lawgiver by which some or all of the

---

[41] The conditions usually given for a radical sanation are: 1) the convalidation of the marriage; 2) the legitimation of the offspring; 3) the spiritual good of the petitioner, and 4) the cessation of concubinage.

[42] Payen, *De Matrimonio in Missionibus*, II, n. 2600; Gasparri, *De Matrimonio*, II, n. 1209 ff.; Harrigan, p. 65ff.; Capello, *De Sacramentis*, V, *De Matrimonio*, n. 851.

[43] Cf. preceding chapter.

[44] *Legitimacy and Legitimation*, The Catholic University of America Canon Law Studies, n. 138 (Washington, D.C.; The Catholic University of America Press, 1941), p. 44.

rights and honors of legitimacy are conferred on an illegitimate child."[45]

A brief analysis of the definition of Vermeersch-Creusen will serve to emphasize what the product of the fiction of the law is in accord with the ruling enacted in canon 1138, §1. First, legitimation is a benefit. This is obvious; by legitimation there is acknowledged for the recipient a status that he previously lacked, a new status that negates his former state of ignominy. Secondly, this benefit may come from either the law or the lawgiver. The legitimation may be the result of a law. In this case the functioning of the law would automatically produce the effect of legitimation. Such is the case in radical sanation. The legitimation in this case is effected indirectly by the enactment of the law. Or the legitimation may be granted by the lawgiver. In this instance the legislator through an edict effects the legitimation of the beneficiary. Such is the case in legitimation by Papal rescript. The legitimation in this case is effected directly, as the legislator acts directly upon the recipient of the legitimation. Finally, some or all of the rights and honors of legitimacy are conferred on an illegitimate child. Whether the legitimation will carry with it a full or a partial bestowal of rights and honors depends upon the manner of the legitimation. These rights and honors had previously been denied the beneficiary because of his juridic stigma of illegitimacy. Now, with legitimation, the recipient becomes juridically equal (in some or in all of these rights and honors) with those who enjoyed legitimacy from birth.

With reference to the element of legitimation one should properly understand who can become the recipients of legitimation. Those who lack legitimacy (*filii illegitimi*) are the offspring born in conditions other than they are delineated in canon 1114.[46] As this canon provides, whether by implication or directly, the offspring may be illegitimate because of two reasons: 1. because during the period lapsing from the conception to th birth of the child the parents were not joined in a juridically efficacious or putative marriage, and 2. because, although the child was

---

[45] *Epitome Iuris Canonici*, II, n. 419, "Legitimatio est beneficium legis aut Principlis quo iura et honores legitimitatis, sive quadam sive omnia, filio illegitimo conferuntur."

[46] "Legitimi sunt filii concept aut nati ex matrimonio valido vel putativo, nisi parentibus ob solemnem professionem religiosam vel susceptum ordinem prohbitus tempore conceptionis fuerit usus matrimonii antea contracti."

conceived in and of a valid union, the use of the conjugal rights, by the parents joined in a valid union was by positive law prohibited at the time of the child's conception. This latter case would be exemplified if, when the conception of the child occurred, the parents were prohibited the use of their marital rights because of a solemn profession or the reception of Sacred Orders.

Legitimation is very evident in the canonical history of the Church. The problems caused and the questions raised by legitimation have been the object of intensive study and extensive writings by scholars of various ages.[47] It is not the intent of the writer to delve deeply into the question of legitimation as such. This investigation is done *ex professo* by the authors here cited. The writer intends merely to give a summary sketch of the different types of legitimation in canon law, in order properly to present legitimation by radical sanation in particular.

In addition to legitimation by way of a radical sanation there are three other types of legitimation employed in canon law. These three types are: 1) legitimation by subsequent marriage of the parents; 2) legitimation by dispensation, and 3) legitimation by papal rescript.[48]

Legitimation through the subsequent marriage of the parents is dealt with in canon 1116.[49] The text of this canon appears self-evident, and very little commentary is required. The subsequent marriage may be either true or putative, and it may be either a new contract or a convalidation of a previously invalid union. The subsequent marriage need not be consummated. Brennan, Capello and Payen add that there need not be any possibility for the consummating of the

[47] *Supra*, p. 8 ff.; McDevitt, *Legitimacy and Legitimation*, p. 11 ff.; Genestal, *Histoire de la Legitimation des Enfants Naturels en Droit Canonique (Parisiis*, 1905); Bernhard, "*La Sanatio in Radice* et la Legitimation des Enfants, dans la Doctrine Canonique Moderene, Revue de Droit Canonique (Strasbough), 1951—), II (1952), 30-56; Ciprotti, "De Prole Legitima vel illegitima in Iure Canonico Vigenti," *Apollinaris (Romaae*, 1928—), XII (1939), 329-347; 490-519.

[48] McDevitt, *Legitimacy and Legitimation*, p. 124; Harrigan, p. 50; Payen, *De Matrimonio in Missionibus*, II, n. 2173; Vermeersch-Creusen, *Epitome Iuris Canonici*, II, n. 421.

[49] "Per subsequens parentum matrimonium sive verum sive putativum, sive noviter contractum sive convalidatum, etiam non consummation, legitima efficitur proles, dummodo parentes habiles stiterint ad matrimonium inter se contrahendum tempore conceptionis, vel praegnationis, vel nativitatis."

marriage.[50] The parents need to have been juridically capable (*habiles*) of entering a valid union with each other either at the time of the conception, during the period of the gestation, or at the time of the birth of the child. The child to be legitimated may have been born as the product of fornication or of concubinage. These antecedents do not affect the legitimation provided that the parents were juridically capable of intermarriage at any of the three times mentioned in the canon. Thus the canon refers only to natural children, as they are called (*filii naturales*). A child conceived in adultery or incest could by the subsequent marriage of its parents be legitimated provided, respectively, that before his birth the true husband had died, or a dispensation had removed the impediment of consanguinity or affinity.[51] In these cases the parents would be juridically capable of intermarriage at the time of the child's birth. The subsequent marriage must be between the parents of the child. This demand seems to be rather evident from the text of the canon itself (*inter se*).[52]

Legitimation by dispensation is treated in canon 1051.[53] Canon 1116 provided only for the legitimation of *natural children.* Thus children whose parents were not free to enter a valid marriage at the time of the children's conception, during the period of their gestation, or at the time of their birth, cannot profit by legitimation as deriving through their parents' subsequent marriage. Canon 1051 provides for some of the offspring who are outside the scope of canon 1116, and legitimates them by way of dispensation. Adulterine and sacrilegious children are excluded from legitimation by way of dispensation, but some other types of spurious offspring can be legitimated in virtue of canon 1051. (Cf. canon 1076, §3.) The following division of

---

[50] *Simple Convalidation,* p. 109; *De Matrimonio,* n. 750; *De Matrimonio in Missionibus,* II, n. 2176.

[51] Payen, *De Matrimonio in Missionibus,* II, n. 2173, §1; McDevitt, *Legitimacy* and *Legitimation,* p. 132; Harrigan, p. 52.

[52] Payen, *De Matrimonio in Missionibus,* II, n. 2175; McDevitt, *Legitimacy and Legitimation,* p. 125; Harrington, p. 52.

[53] "Per dispensationem super impedimento dirimente concessam sive ex potestate ordinaria, sive expotestate delegata per indultum generale, non vero per rescriptum in casibus particularibus, conceditur quoque eo ipso legitimatio prolis, si qua iis cum quibus dispensatur iam nata vel concepta fuerit, excepta tamen adulterina et sacrilega."

illegitimate so-called spurious children is employed by many authors[54] and proves helpful in any consideration given to canon 1051.

1. Simply spurious children—these are the illegitimate offspring who do not belong to any of the following types of spurious offspring. They are not adulterine, sacrilegious, incestuous or nefarious children.

2. Adulterine—these are the children whose parents, either one or both, were bound by the impediment of ligamen (prior bond of marriage) at the time of the childrens' conception and birth.

3. Sacrilegious—these are the children whose parents, either one or both, were bound at the time of the children's conception and birth by the diriment impediment of solemn religious profession, or whose father was subject to the impediment of a Sacred Order; also sacrilegious are those children whose parents, at the time of the children's conception, were prohibited the use of all marital rights because of the solemn profession of at least one parent or the reception of a Sacred Order by the husband.[55]

4. Incestuous—these are the illegitimate offspring who are conceived and born of a union of two parties prohibited at the time of the conception and birth of the children from intermarriage within the degrees of consanguinity in the collateral line or within the degrees of affinity in either the direct or collateral line delineated in canons 1076, §2, and 1077.

Nefarious—these are the illegitimate children who are the evil product of a union in which the parents are related in the direct line of consanguinity.[56]

As was noted above, adulterine and sacrilegious children are explicitly excluded from the benefit of legitimation by way of dispensation. Nefarious children are likewise excluded, for no dispensation could remove the impediment of consanguinity in the direct line.[57] Their parents

---

[54] Gasparri, *De Matrimonio,* II, n. 1112; Harrigan, p. 53; Payen, *De Matrimonio in Missionibus,* II, n. 2162; Wernz-Vidal, *Ius Matrimoniale,* n. 608; Capello, *De Sacramentis,* V, *DeMatrimonio,* n. 745.

[55] Cf. canon 1114.

[56] In classifying the various types of children as adulterine, sacrilegious, incestuous or nefarious the writer obviously means that these illegitimate children result from adultery, sacrilege, incest or incest in the direct line of consanguinity.

[57] Cf. canon 1076, §3.

could never be thought of as being juridically capable of intermarriage. Incestuous children resulting from parents related to each other in the first degree of consanguinity in the collateral line are also excluded from the benefit of legitimation by way of dispensation in accordance with the ruling enacted in canon 1051. This exclusion obtains in view of the possibility that this impediment is one of the divine law.[58]

The illegitimate offspring then who can be legitimated by way of dispensation, as intimated in canon 1051, are the simply spurious and incestuous offspring (excepting the cases listed above). These children become legitimated by the dispensation from the diriment impediment that caused their parents to be juridically incapable of intermarriage during the period lapsing from the conception to the birth of the children concerned. The dispensation, however, must have been granted in virtue of ordinary power or of delegated power derived through a general indult. If the bishop were to obtain the dispensation by rescript for a particular case, this rescript would not automatically include the legitimation of the offspring. This dispensation must indeed have been granted in compliance with the terms of canon 1051.

The third manner of legitimation looks to the issuance of a papal rescript. This manner of legitimation is broader in scope than any of the other methods of legitimation. This is so because no illegitimate child is absolutely barred from legitimation through the power of the Pope. However, this manner of legitimation is perhaps used less frequently than any of the other types of legitimation, for it is obtained only when specifically petioned.[59] Obviously, legitimation by papal rescript is very advantageous for those illegitimate children whose parents never do contract marriage. By this means of legitimation they are able to gain what was denied them by their parents' failure to marry. Since the legitimation is effected by rescript, the extent of the legitimation in regard to the canonical effects must be learned from the tenor of the rescript in each case. Although the Holy Father can legitimate any child—be he natural or spurious—by this method, there are certain types of illegitimates to whom he does not customarily grant legitimation. Payen stated that the Pope scarcely ever legitimates children born of adultery, sacrilege or incest in the direct line, and Gas-

---

[58] *Supra*, p. 62.

[59] Wernz-Vidal, *Ius Matrimoniale*, n. 615; Harrigan, p. 57.

parri stated that the Pope never legitimates illegitimates who are the evil fruit of sacrilege.[60] Harrigan adds, however, that the petition should be made in these cases also, since the legitimation depends entirely upon the free will of the Pontiff.[61]

Upon this cursory consideration of legitimation in general, namely by way of subsequent marriage, by way of dispensation, and by way of papal rescript, legitimation by way of radical sanation can now be treated specifically.

Article V. Legitimation by Radical Sanation

Payen spoke of radical sanation as an objective convalidation of a marriage on the strength of the prior consent, and moreover as a retroaction, through a fiction of the law to the past in respect to the canonical effects, and therefore especially concerning the legitimation of the offspring.[62] This description of a *sanatio in radice* by Payen brings out very well the distinction between the convalidation and the legitimation that is contained in a radical sanation. The convalidation is something what is true, or objective, and as such it can only occur *ex nunc*. The retroactive legitimation as such is something that relies upon a fiction of the law. While in reality only being true *ex nunc*, it is reputed as true from the inception of the *radix*. This distinction between the true and fictitious effects of a radical sanation explains how in a sanation improperly so-called the fictitious retroactive legitimation is effected without the actual convalidation of the union.

As has been stated earlier in this work,[63] radical sanation improperly so-called may be employed when one of the parties is insane or deceased. In the consideration of such a use, it becomes rather evident that legitimation by radical sanation improperly so-called closely resembles legitimation by Papal rescript. In both cases the only effect produced is the legitimation of the offspring. In radical sanation improperly so-called there is no convalidation effected, because there is no invalid union present to convalidate. Nor is there a dispensation from the law of

---

[60] Payen, *De Matrimonio in Missionibus,* II, n. 2173, §4; Gasparri, *De Matrimonio,* II, n. 1121.

[61] *The Radical Sanation of Invalid Marriages,* p. 57.

[62] *De Matrimoni in Missionibus,* II, n. 2595.

[63] *Supra,* p. 55.

the renewal of consent, since there is no mutual abiding consent present. Since the convalidation is not possible, there is no dispensation from the impediment (if there be any) that invalidated the original union. Hence, the only effect is the legitimation of the offspring.[64]

Despite the close resemblance between legitimation by radical sanation improperly so-called and legitimation by Papal rescript there is an essential difference between the two. Although legitimation is the only effect of each of them, they differ as to how this legitimation is accomplished.[65] Legitimation by Papal rescript is effected directly by means of the rescript, whereas legitimation by radical sanation improperly so-called is produced indirectly as a result of the favor of radical sanation.

In order to examine the extent of legitimation by radical sanation a twofold division of the extent will facilitate the examination considerably. First the writer intends to treat the legitimation in regard to the recipients of it and then to examine it in regard to the degree of its plentitude.

Section 1. Recipients of the Legitimation

The first subjects of legitimation by radical sanation to be considered are in reality not illegitimate at all. These subjects are the offspring of a putative marriage. The law expressly states that such children are legitimate.[66] Although the children of a putative marriage do not enjoy a state of absolute legitimacy, since that state is proper only to the offspring of a valid marriage, they nevertheless do enjoy a state of juridical legitimacy in virtue of the Code.[67] Then despite the fact that they are already legitimate, these children receive another title to legitimation when the putative (but objectively invalid) marriage is the object of a radical sanation.[68]

The fact that radical sanation gives another title of legitimation to children of a putative marriage seems to be verified by the follow-

---

[64] Payen, *De Matrimonio in Missionibus,* II, n. 2607.

[65] Harrigan, p. 59.

[66] Canon 1114.

[67] McDevitt, *Legitimacy and Legitimation,* p. 175.

[68] Gasparri, *De Matrimonio,* II, n. 1209; McDevitt, *Legitimacy and Legitimation,* p. 175; Harrigan, p. 65; Wernz-Vidal, *Ius Matrimoniale,* n. 671.

ing act of the Holy See. It is known that The Sacred Poenitentiary has granted a radical sanation *ad cautelam* for what is perhaps a putative marriage. In doing so express mention was made in the grant to the effect that the fact of the sanation should be inscribed in the parish matrimonial register. The purpose of this directive was that in case of future question or attack the legitimacy of the offspring as well as the validity of the marriage would stand.[69]

In regard to whether or not natural children[70] are possible subjects of legitimation by radical sanation, a distinction must be made. If the natural child is born of fornication or concubinage at a time when no true marital, naturally sufficient consent existed on the part of the parents, legitimation by radical sanation will not be effected. The reason is that the *radix* of the invalid union had not begun to exist at the time of the child's birth. However, since the parents were free to contract a valid marriage at the time of the birth of the offspring, the child will not be denied legitimation. In this event the child will be made legitimate by the subsequent marriage of his parents.[71] If the natural child is born after the parents have exchanged a true marital consent, he will benefit from legitimation by radical sanation. The *radix* of the union in this case pre-dates the birth of the child. Similar to a child born of a sanated putative marriage, a natural child born

---

[69] Petition—"Titius et Caia. matrimonio, invalido, uti videtur, coniuncti, post baptismum, sub conditione reiteratum, consensum renovarunt coram sacerdote at sine testibus. Cum sine gravissimo incommodo Titius et Caia, qui in bona fide sunt, adigi nequeant ad denuo renovandum consensum, et huiusmodi consensus perseveret, petitur ad cautelam, sanatio in radice dicti matrimonii."

Response—"Sacra Paenitentiaria, de speciali et expressa Apostolica Auctoritate, benigne sic annuente SSmo Domino Nostro Pio PP. XII, matrimonium, de quo in praefatis litteris, sic uti exponitur forte nulliter contractum, dummodo prior perseveret consensus, in radice sanat et convalidat ad cautelam. pro foro conscientiae, ita tamen ut huiusmodi sanatio in foro quoque externo suffragetur. Ad quem effectum huiusmodi sanatio notetur in margine prima inscriptionis matrimoniorum in libro parochiali, servando caute in paroechiali Archivo et praesentes litteras, expressis in earum calce nominibus, cognominibus ac patria coniugum, ut pro quocumque futuro eventu de matrimoni validitate et prolis legitimatate constare possit." The foregoing text is an example of a grant of a radical sanation by the Sacred Poenitentiary.

[70] *Supra,* p. 108.

[71] McDevitt, *Legitimacy and Legitimation,* p. 177; Harrigan, p. 61; Ciprotti, *Apollinaris,* XII (1939), 514.

after the inception of the *radix* of the invalid union will enjoy a twofold title to legitimacy. This twofold title will be legitimation by radical sanation and legitimation by subsequent marriage.[72]

The same distinction that was made in view of the presence of a true marital consent of the parents in relation to the time of birth in regard to natural children is also applicable to merely spurious children.[73] If the merely spurious child was born before the parents exchanged true marital consent, the offspring will not be a recipient of legitimation by retroaction contained in a radical sanation. However, the offspring in question will be legitimated by the dispensation according to canon 1051, contained in the grant of a radical sanation. The fact that the dispensation from the diriment impediment is contained in the grant of the radical sanation does not diminish the force of the dispensation in regard to effecting legitimation in virtue of canon 1051. The legitimation, however, will be effected only if the radical sanation is granted in virtue of ordinary power, or of delegated held power through a general indult.[74] Harrigan says that in this case the legitimation will be effected only *ex nunc*.[75] Ciprotti, on the other hand, states that since the dispensation contained in a radical sanation is granted *ad praeteritum* through a fiction of law, then it follows that the legitimation will be effected *ex tunc*.[76]

Legitimation by the dispensation contained in a radical sanation is effected only if the impediment is present when the sanation its granted. If the impediment has ceased, then there is not contained in the grant any dispensation, and hence no legitimation by dispensation.

Incestuous children are,[77] with the exception of the offspring of par-

---

[72] Harrigan, *loc. cit.*

[73] *Supra*, p. 109.

[74] Cf. can. 1138, §1, and can. 1051; McDevitt, *Legitimacy and Legitimation*, p. 177; Harrigan, pp. 61-62; Ciprotti, *Apollinaris*, XII (1939), 514.

[75] *The Radical Sanation of Invalid Marriages*, p. 62.

[76] Ciprotti, *loc. cit.*: "Quodsi proles sit spuria, seu desit requisita parentum habilitas, fit legitimatio ex dispensatione, ad norman can. 1051 (nisi sanatio in radice concessa sit ex potestate delegata ad casum particularem), quia dispensatio, ut diximus, censetur, per iuris fictionem, concessa statim ante momentum ad quod fit retrotractio; dummodo tamen eo momento adhuc ad fuerit impedimentum."

[77] *Supra*, p. 109.

ents who are brother and sister, in the same category as merely spurious children in regard to legitimation by radical sanation. If the incestuous child is not legitimated by the retroaction contained in radical sanation, but rather only by the dispensation (can. 1051 and can. 1138, §1). If the birth follows upon the inception of the *radix,* the offspring is legitimated by radical sanation.[78] In his study Harrigan fails to exclude incestuous offspring whose parents are related in the first degree of consanguinity of the collateral[79] line. Such children would not benefit from legitimation by radical sanation, for since the impediment involved is a doubtful impediment of the divine positive law, no sanation would be granted in such an instance.[80]

Sacriligious offspring[81] also are potential recipients of legitimation through a radical sanation. Since Sacred Orders and solemn religious profession are impediments of merely ecclesiastical law,[82] there is no doubt of this conclusion (can. 1139, §1). This statement is true in regard to both categories of sacrilegious children. That is, those at least one of whose parents, during the entire period from conception to birth, is bound by a diriment impediment of Sacred Orders or solemn religious profession,[83] or who are conceived of a valid marriage (contracted prior to the reception of Sacred Orders or the making of solemn religious profession) while the use of the marital rights of their parents are prohibited by positive law because of Sacred Orders or solemn religious profession (can. 1114).

Harrigan states that while sacrilegious children can be legitimated by radical sanation, the Church is not accustomed to bestowing this type of legitimation upon them. Thus since these offspring would not be legitimated by a radical sanation granted to their parents, their only

---

78 Cf. preceding footnote, 77.

79 *Op. cit.,* 61-62.

80 Cf. *supra,* p. 62 ff.

81 *Supra,* p. 109.

82 *Supra,* p. 66.

83 The simple vows of chastity of the Society of Jesus is a diriment impediment and is governed by canon 1073. Gregorius XIII, const. *Ascendente Domino,* 5 maii 1584, Fontes, n. 153. Authorities, however, do not include offspring born of a marriage invalidated by this simple vow as being sacrilegious. Cf. Gasparri, *De Matrimonio,* II, n. 1112; Wernz-Vidal, *Ius Matrimoniale,* n. 608; Payen, *De Matrimonio in Missionibus,* II, n. 2162.

recourse for legitimation is through rescript of the Pope.[84] There does not appear to be any basis for this statement. Payen, McDevitt and Ciprotti all reject it.[85] They state that unless the rescript expressly provides otherwise, the sacrilegious children are legitimated by radical sanation. This latter opinion certainly seems to be the more reasonable of the two. There is nothing in the law that would exclude these children from legitimation by radical sanation. Since the retroactive legitimation is by law a constituent part of the grant of radical sanation, there is no apparent cause why the Church would withhold this effect when a radical sanation is granted to parties who have sacrilegious offspring.

Adulterine children[86] are excluded from the benefit of legitimation by radical sanation. The reason for this exclusion is obvious. The offspring were conceived and born at a time when the impediment of *ligamen* existed. Ligamen is a diriment impediment of the positive divine law,[87] and therefore no radical sanation can be granted in the face of this impediment.[88]

Nefarious children likewise are excluded from being recipients of legitimation by radical sanation even in the improper sense.[89] The reason here also is obvious. For consanguinity in the first degree of the direct line is a diriment impediment of the divine law; and consanguinity in any of the other degrees of the direct line is, at least doubtfully, a diriment impediment of the divine law.[90] Therefore no radical sanation is ever granted in the case of this impediment.

Section 2. Degree of Plentitude of the Legitimation

Authors divide legitimation in general into three classes in regard to the degree of its plenitude. The first division is called *minus plena legitimatio*. The second type is called *plena legitimatio*. And the

---

[84] P. *Op. cit.*, p. 64.

[85] Payen, *De Matrimonio in Missionibus*, II, n. 2173; McDevitt, *Legitimacy and Legitimation*, p. 178; Ciprotti, *Apollinaris*, XII (1939), 514.

[86] *Supra*, p. 109.

[87] *Supra*, p. 62.

[88] Can. 1139, §2; also cf. *supra*, p. 63.

[89] *Supra*, p. 108.

[90] *Supra*, p. 62 ff.

third category is termed *legitimatio plenissima.*[91] The first or lowest degree of legitimation is the type in which some of the rights and honors proper to one who is absolutely legitimate are given to the recipient. This type of legitimation is usually obtained by way of papal rescript. The rights and honors withheld vary according to the tenor of the individual rescript.[92]

Legitimatio plena is the kind of legitimation that is ordinarily granted. This type of legitimation bestows upon the recipient all of the rights and honors proper to the state of absolute legitimacy, with the exception however of such things which are expressly withheld.[93]

The final type, that of a most complete legitimation, is termed *legitimatio plenissima.* It is this type of legitimation that is conferred upon an illegitimate through a radical sanation.[94] It is now the writer's purpose to consider the force of this *legitimatio plenissima* of a radical sanation. It must be stressed that no matter how complete the legitimation which is conferred by a radical sanation may be, it is still a juridic legitimation. Absolute legitimacy results only when a child is born of a valid marriage. Juridic legitimacy, despite its degree of plenitude, can never be equal to absolute legitimacy.[95]

In order to ascertain the full extent of the state of legitimation conferred by way of a radical sanation, one may well approach the topic in a negative manner. In this way the rights and honors denied to one who is illegitimate will be presented, and then the question of whether or not these rights and honors are bestowed upon the recipient of legitimation through a radical sanation can be duly considered.

According to law the following prerogatives and dignities are denied to one who is illegitimate: 1) admission to the seminary;[96] 2) the

---

[91] Payen, *De Matrimonio in Missionibus,* II, nn. 2600, 2172; Harrigan, pp. 65-66; Capello, *De Sacramentis,* V, *De Matrimonio,* n. 752; McDevitt, *Legitimacy and Legitimation,* p. 46.

[92] Cappello, *loc. cit.;* McDevitt, *loc. cit.;* Gasparri, *De Matrimonio,* n. 1121.

[93] Canon 1117; Harrigan, p. 66; McDevitt, *op. cit.,* pp. 137 ff.

[94] Payen, *De Matrimonio in Missionibus,* II, n. 2600; McDevitt, *Legitimacy and Legitimation,* p. 182 ff.; Wernz-Vidal, *Ius Matrimoniale,* n. 671; Harrigan, p. 66; Cappello, *De Sacramentis, V, De Matrimonio,* n. 851.

[95] McDevitt, *op. cit.,* pp. 64 ff.; Bastnagel, "Legitimate Status for High Dignitaries," *The Jurist,* VIII (1948), 219-222.

[96] Canon 1363, §1.

reception of Orders;[97] 3) the office of major superior in religion,[98]; 4) the dignity of abbott or prelate *nullius;*[99] 5) the dignity of the episcopacy;[100] and, finally, the dignity of the cardinalate.[101]

There is no problem concerning the first two prerogatives mentioned (admission to the seminary and the reception of Orders). Any doubt at all in regard to the rightful bestowing of them upon those who were legitimated by radical sanation was dispelled by the Code Commission in a response on July 13, 1930. The Code Commission in reply to the question whether sons who were legitimated by the subsequent marriage of their parents were to be considered as meeting the requirements of canon 1363, §1, answered in the affirmative.[102]

Since legitimation by way of a radical sanation is in effect fundamentally at least equivalent to legitimation through the subsequent intermarriage of the parents, though actually the former contains a fuller degree of legitimation,[103] this response of the Code Commission is, at least in effect, applicable. Also from this same response the bestowal of the requisite qualifications for the receiving of Orders may be proved. Since one who receives his legitimation through radical sanation is considered as a fit entrant for the seminary, it follows that this same individual will be accepted as a fit recipient for Orders. It would be most illogical to accept the juridical legitimation received through a radical sanation as qualifying one for the seminary, and then later on in the course at the seminary to rule that this status did not qualify one to receive Orders.

Canon 1117[104] definitely states that those who are legitimated through a subsequent marriage are equal in all things regarding canonical effects with those who are legitimate, except where there is an express provision to the contrary. Now, there is no express provision in either canon 1363, §1, or in canon 948, §1, that would exclude chil-

[97] Canon 948, §1.

[98] Canon 504.

[99] Canon 320, §2.

[100] Canon 331, §1, 1°.

[101] Canon 232, §2, 1°.

[102] *AAS,* XII (1930), 365; Bouscaren, *Canon Law Digest,* I, 661.

[103] McDevitt, *Legitimacy and Legitimation,* p. 191.

[104] "Filii legitimati per subsequens matrimonium, ad effectus canonicos quod attinet, in omnibus aequiparantur legitimis, nisi aliud expresse cautum fuerit."

dren legitimated by radical sanation from entering the seminary or receiving orders. Thus there appears to be no basis whatsoever for denying the qualifications required by canons 1363, §1, and 984, §1; in fact, the provision of the law is explicit to this effect. The text of canon 1117 amounts to a positive disposition of law in favor of their being responsive to these requirements.[105]

Both Harrigan and McDevitt, in dealing with the effects of legitimation through radical sanation, fail to mention canon 504. The canon requires that, in order to be qualified for the office of major superior, one must be born of a legitimate marriage, "*ex legitimo matrimonio natus.*" The silence of these two authors seems to indicate that both accept this type of legitimation as qualifying one for the office of major superior. This conclusion appears especially true in view of the discussion which both present in regard to the requisites of legitimacy as established in canons 320, §2, 331, §1 Ø1, and 232, §2 Ø1.[106] Woywod and Bouscaren-Ellis explicity state that legitimation by radical sanation does qualify one to be a major superior. Bowe also is of the same opinion.[107] The view of Bastnagel requires the same degree of legitimacy for the office of major superior that is demanded for the dignities of abbots and prelates *nullius,* of bishops, and of cardinals. Since he regards legitimation by way of a radical sanation as an insufficient qualification in respect to the latter three dignities, he also denies that legitimation by way of a radical sanation qualifies one in regard to the requirement of legitimacy in the office of major superior.[108]

The writer inclines toward the positive view, that is, that legitimation by way of a radical sanation suffices to qualify one for the office of major superior. The phrase "born of a legitimate wedlock" in canon 504 does not seem to offer an express provision to the contrary that would bar those who are legitimated through the subsequent intermarriage of their parents, not to speak of the legitimation granted in a radical sanation. The legislator is very definite in his manner of

---

[105] Cappello, *De Sacramentis,* IV, *De Sacra Ordinatione,* n. 462.

[106] McDevitt, *Legitimacy and Legitimation,* pp. 183 ff.; Harrigan, pp. 67 ff.

[107] Woywod, *A Practical Commentary on the Code of Canon Law* (2 vols., New York, 1925), I, 186; Bouscaren-Ellis, *Canon Law,* p. 240; Bowe, *Religious Superioresses,* The Catholic University of America Canon Law Studies, n. 228 (Washington, D.C.; The Catholic University of America Press, 1946), p. 74.

[108] *The Jurist,* VIII (1948), 219-222.

excluding those who are legitimated through a subsequent intermarriage of their parents when he delineates the requisites in candidates for an abbacy *nullius*, a prelacy *nullius*, the episcopacy, and the cardinalate. Had he been of the same mind with reference to the office of major superior as mentioned in canon 504, it seems that he would have been equally as definite. In canon 331, which establishes the requisites in a candidate for the episcopacy, there occurs the same phrase (*"ex legitimo matrimonio"*) that one finds in canon 504. However, in canon 331 the legislator further adds that the candidate must not have become legitimated through a subsequent marriage between his parents.[109] If the expression "legitimate wedlock" in canon 504 included the requisite that the birth had to be of a valid or putative marriage, it would have been quite superfluous to add in canon 331, §1, 1, the phrase that explicitly bars the notion of legitimation through a subsequent marriage. In view of this the writer holds that one who receives his title to legitimation through a radical sanation is qualified in regard to the requirement of legitimate birth, as this requirement is made in canon 504 with reference to prospective major religious superiors.

Upon this consideration of the effect of legitimation by way of a radical sanation with reference to the status of legitimacy as required: 1. for admission to the seminary; 2. for the reception of Orders, and 3. for the office of a major superior in religion, it now remains to study the effect of this type of legitimation in regard to the eligibility for an abbacy or prelacy *nullius*, for the episcopacy, and for the cardinalate.

Bastnagel and Harrigan in their negative view, and McDevitt in his positive stand, have given this question more consideration than the authors customarily give to the topic.[110] These three authors make it quite clear before going into the discussion, that the question is chiefly one of academic or theoretical value, and that there is little practical point to the discussion. The reason is that the Holy See in actual practice grants *ad cautelam* a dispensation from whatever impediments may be existing.

The question seems to hinge a great deal upon whether or not the

---

[109] Canon 331, §1, 1°. "Natus ex legitimo matrimonio, non autem legitimatus etiam per subsequens matrimonium."

[110] Bastnagel, *The Jurist*, VIII (1948), 219-222; Harrigan, pp. 67-71; McDevitt, *Legitimacy and Legitimation*, pp. 183-191.

exceptions incorporated in canon 1117 apply to legitimation by radical sanation. Since no ruling has been given on this question, the matter is open to discussion and argumentation. If the exceptive clause in canon 1117 refers to radical sanation, then one who is legitimated in this fashion does not qualify for the three dignities in question. On the other hand, if the exceptive clause in canon 1117 is not applicable to radical sanation, then the one who has received his title to legitimation through a sanation is eligible for these dignities.

Most authors proclaim the fullness of the legitimation enacted through a radical sanation, but they do not mention explicitly the question concerning the eligibility for an abbacy or prelacy *nullius,* for the episcopacy, or for the cardinalate. Gasperri and Wernz-Vidal stated that a *sanatio* makes the offspring *habilis quoad omnes effectus canonicos,* but they do not elaborate upon their statement.[111] Ciprotti, Payen and Cappello state that the offspring legitimated by radical sanation obtain all the effects of legitimacy and therefore are not bound by the exceptions in canon 1117. De Smet's view was much the same though he did not expressly advert to canon 1117.[112] These authors appear to take an affirmative view in the matter of eligibility. However, the terseness of Gasparri and Wernz-Vidal in this regard makes it rather difficult to cite them as supporting either view.

Harrigan and Bastnagel offer as their first argument against the proposion that legitimation through a radical sanation answers to the requisites set for the three dignities in question the following: they concede that a radical sanation gives to the one legitimated the fullness of legitimacy. However, no matter how complete this legitimacy may be, it nevertheless is still only a juridic legitimacy. Now, the canons in question contain nothing that would indicate that they demand anything less than absolute legitimacy, or the especial legitimacy proper to one born of a putative marriage. The fact that a radical sanation bestows the fullness of juridic legitimacy upon the recipient does not mean that this legitimacy is not restricted by the Holy See. The canons in question seem quite clear in stressing the demand that the candidate

[111] *De Matrimonio,* II, n. 1213; *Ius Matrimoniale,* n. 671.

[112] Ciprotti, *Apollinaris,* XII (1939), 515; Payen, *De Matrimonio in Missionibus,* II, n. 2600; Cappello, *De Sacramentis* V, *De Matrimonio,* n. 857; DeSmet, *De Sponsalibus et Matrimonio,* n. 736, note 1, n. 291, 2^{0}, note 6.

be born of a valid or putative marriage. This is an objective requirement. The fact that, through a fiction of the law, one legitimated by radical sanation is construed as though he were the product of a valid marriage does not seem sufficient.

Harrigan then appeals to the Constitution *Postquam* of Pope Sixtus V.[113] This document treats of the requirements in regard to legitimacy for Cardinals. Harrigan claims that though Sixtus V did not mention radical sanation by name, the fact that he excluded legitimation through subsequent marriage and other means of legitimation implied that he also excluded legitimation by way of a radical sanation as qualifying one for the cardinalate. Harrigan says that since Sixtus V was not without knowledge of radical sanation and its effects, and yet made no privilege to those legitimated in such a manner, he also wished to bar them from the cardinalate. Harrigan states that since the laws regarding the cardinalate are so similar to the laws regarding the other dignities in question the same reasons prevail. In addition he cites the Constitution *Onus Apostolicae,* of Pope Gregory XIV which demanded that bishops and lower prelates be born of a legitimate marriage.[114] Harrigan rests his argument on the fact that objective and absolute legitimacy are required for the offices under discussion, whereas, a radical sanation confers only a juridical title to legitimacy. Bastnagel also holds that these dignities demand a state of absolute legitimacy, and that therefore radical sanation cannot supply the required title to legitimacy.

McDevitt rejects the negative view as expostulated by Harrigan,

---

[113] 3 Dec. 1586, §12: "Praeterea, qui Cardinales creandi erunt, legitimis, et honestis sint exorti natalibus, neque ulla prorsus labe, aut illegitimorum natalium suspicione quovis modo laborent, sed omni macula, et impuritate careant, alioquin ad tam eminentem dignitatis gradum, penitus inhabiles, et illius incapaces sint, et esse censeantur . . . Ideo ut puriori dignitati puriores natales respondeant, quoscumque illegitime natos, . . . etiam genitos ex soluto, et soluta, inter quos tunc Matrimonium, etiam rite, et solemniter in facie Ecclesiae contractum, vel alias legitimatos, et quomodolibet habilitatos, et natalibus restitutos, ac quorumvis bonorum capaces effectos, etiam si cum eis, ut hanc ipsam dignitatem obtinere valeant, super defectu natalium fuerit expresse, et in specie auctoritate Apostolica quomodolibet dispensatum, nihilominus praedictae Cardinalatus dignitatis prorsus incapaces, et ad eam obtinendam perpetuo inhabiles decernimus, ac declaramus."—*Fontes,* n. 159.

[114] 15 maii, 1591, §§9, 12; *Fontes,* n. 171.

and gives the following reasons for the affirmative view: 1) in the Constitution *Postquam* there is no express mention of the ones legitimated by radical sanation as being excluded from the cardinalate; 2) the words *alias legitimatos etc.,* are in themselves not enough to show that this document excludes the ones legitimated by radical sanation. Since the latter are considered as though they were born of a valid marriage, explicit mention should have been made if they were to be barred; 3) canon 232, §2 Ø1 excludes from the dignity those who are legitimated through a subsequent marriage, but it does not mention those who are legitimated by radical sanation, and these latter enjoy a fuller title to legitimacy than do the former; 4) canon 1117 cannot be used as a norm to determine the extent of legitimation by radical sanation, for the effects of radical sanation are expressly stated in canon 1138, §1; 5) authors do not mention the ones legitimated by radical sanation as being excluded from the dignity of the cardinalate; and 6) legitimation is a favor, and so must be given the widest possible interpretation consistent with the law.

Having seen the two sides of the question, the writer inclines toward the affirmative view as given by McDevitt. The crux of the matter seems reducible to this issue: is the fictional title of legitimacy that is received through a radical sanation and which construes the offspring as though he were born of a valid marriage equal to the objective and absolute title to legitimacy that one born of a valid marriage enjoys? The equality, of course, is concerned only with the requisites for the dignities in question.

If the ones legitimated through a radical sanation are bound by the exceptive clause in canon 1117, it is very difficult to see how this type of legitimation differs from legitimation through a subsequent marriage. Previously a distinction was made to the effect that legitimation through a subsequent marriage bestowed a *plena legitimatio* upon the recipient, whereas legitimation by radical sanation bestowed a *plenissima legitimatio* upon the one receiving it. Now, if both of these types of legitimated offspring are bound by the identical restrictions, such a distinction is futile. Why should the authors state that the ones legitimated are *habiles* in regard to all canonical effects[115] if they are restricted by the exceptive clause in canon 1117? Certainly legitima-

---

[115] *Supra*, p. 117.

tion through a radical sanation is an especial type of legitimation.[116]

The canons that refer to the dignities in question explicitly exclude those who have been legitimated through a subsequent marriage. Yet none of these canons explicitly mentions legitimation by radical sanation. This omission seemingly indicates that the legislator did not wish to exclude the recipients of this latter form of legitimation. Admittedly the canons do require that the candidate must be born of a valid marriage, but it is not stated that this must be an objective birth giving absolute legitimacy. The juridic legitimacy conferred on the one legitimated by radical sanation, whereby he is considered as though he were born of a valid marriage, certainly is not excluded by the canons.

In view of the reasons offered for the affirmative and negative views on the matter discussed above, the writer decides in favor of the affirmative view. He does so in the realization of the fact that the problem is at the moment undecided. There are sound arguments for both sides, and the Holy See has not ruled in favor of either position. The doubt that exists in this matter seems to dictate that the affirmative view be held in order that the offspring in question may receive the benefit of that doubt. Since these persons have not incurred the stigma of illegitimacy through any fault of their own, it does not seem fitting to deprive them of the possibility of the dignities listed above, since there is a probable doubt in their favor.

In addition to the ecclesiastical effects of legitimation by radical sanation, there is also the question of civil effects. This question has little practical import today. During former periods of history this problem was one of great moment.[117] All admit that this legitimation would carry with it civil effects in territories belonging to the Holy See.[118] However, since the seizure of the Papal States in 1860 the Holy See has been practically non-existent as a temporal power. Harrigan expresses the situation very well as it exists today. Although the Holy See can indirectly grant legitimation for civil effects through its

[116] "Legitimatio prolis per sanationem in radice peculiari fit ratione, et ideo praesertim a ceteris distinguitur, quia pleniores habet effectus, cum saepe proles non proprie legitimetur, set legitima omnino fiat per sanationem."—Ciprotti, *Apollinaris*, XII (1939), 512.

[117] Cf. *supra*, p. 4 ff.

[118] Gasparri, *De Matrimonio*, II, n. 1213.

direct legitimation in regard to spiritual effects in lands outside the temporal domain of the Holy See, civil authorities no longer acknowledge this power of the Papacy. Thus, unless some individual state expressly acknowledged this power by reason of a concordat or agreement, there is very little application of these effects of legitimation by radical sanation in regard to the civil law.[119]

Briefly, the following may be said about the fourth juridic effect of the *sanatio in radice;* a radical sanation effects the legitimation of the offspring retroactively to the inception of the *radix* of the union. The children who are legitimated in this fashion may be natural, merely spurious, incestuous (except offspring of parents related in the first degree of consanguinity in the collateral line) or sacrilegious provided they were born after their parents exchanged true marital consent. The title to legitimation effected is a juridic title, but it is so in its most complete sense (legitimatio plenissima). Through this title to legitimation the beneficiary is enabled to receive all of the prerogatives, rights, and dignities that were previously denied him in canon law by reason of his stigma of illegitimacy.

---

119 *The Radical Sanation of Invalid Marriages*, p. 72.

CONCLUSIONS

1. With the grant of the first radical sanation in 1554 the convalidation of the marriage was considered as the chief effect of the *sanatio in radice.*

2. Many pre-Code canonists denied that the dispensation from the law of the renewal of consent was a juridical effect of radical sanation.

3. Many pre-Code canonists held that convalidation by radical sanation was effective retroactively to the first exchange of true marital consent.

4. The fiction of law had its origin in the *Lex Cornelia* of the Roman Law.

5. Convalidation by radical sanation is not to be thought of as being retroactive.

6. Only a *sanatio in radice* improperly so-called can be granted when one of the parties is deceased or permanently insane.

7. Although it is not the common practice of the Church to do so, the Church can grant a *sanatio in radice* after an impediment of the positive or natural divine law has ceased.

8. The dispensation from the law of the renewal of consent verifies the fact that convalidation by way of a radical sanation is a ratification (*ratihabitio*) of the original or previous marital contract.

9. A *sanatio in radice* is valid even though both parties are unwilling to accept it.

10. The element of retroaction in a radical sanation refers to the canonical effects of the marriage, and to the canonical effects alone.

11. Legitimation obtained through a radical sanation renders the recipient responsive to all the qualifications and capable of receiving the rights and dignities of the Church inasmuch as these by law involve the requirement of legitimate status.

BIBLIOGRAPHY

SOURCES

Acta Apostolicae Sedis, Commentarium Officiale, Romae, 1909—.

Acta Sancta Sedis, 41 vols., Romae, 1865-1908.

Bullarii Romani Continuatio Summorum Pontificum, 19 vols., Prati, 1756-1883.

Bruns, Hermann, *Canones Apostolorum et Conciliorum Saeculorum,* IV-VII, 2 vols., Berolini, 1839.

Collectanea S. Congregationis de Propaganda Fide, 2 vols., Romae, 1907.

Codex Iuris Canonici, Pii X Pontificis Maximi iussu digestus, Benedicti Pape XV auctoritate promulgatus, Praefatione, Fontium Annotatione et Indice Analytico-Alphabetico ab Emo Petro Card. Gasparri Auctus, Romae: Typis Polyglottis Vaticanis, 1917; reimpressio, 1946.

Codicis Iuris Canonici Fontes, cura Emi Petri Card. Gasparri ed., 9 vols., Romae (postea Civitate Vaticana): Typis Polyglottis Vaticanis, 1923-1938. (Vols. VII-IX ed. cura et studio Emi Iustiniani Card. Seredi.)

Corpus Iuris Civilis, 3 vols., Berolini, 1928-1929. *Codex Iustinianus,* quem recognovit et retractavit P. Krueger, ed. sterotypa 10, 1929; *Novellae,* quas recognovit R. Schoell, et absolvit G. Kroll, ed, sterotypa 5, 1928.

Hardouin, Jean, Acta Conciliorum et Epistolae Decretales ac Constitutiones Summorum Pontificum, 12 vols., Parisiis, 1714-1715.

Magnum Bullarium Romanum, 19 vols. in 18, Luxemburgi, 1727-1754.

Mansi, Joannes, *Sacrorum Conciliorum Nova et Amplissima Collectio,* 53 vols. in 60, Parisiis, 1901-1927.

Monumenta Germaniae Historica, Legum Sectio III, Concilia, Tomus I, *Concilia Aevi Merovingici,* recensuit Fredericus Maassen, Hannoverae, 1883.

Schroeder, *Canons and Decrees of the Council of Trent, Original Text with English Translations,* St. Louis and London: Herder, 1941.

Synodus Alexandrina Coptorum Habita Cairi in Aegypto, Romae, 1889.

REFERENCE WORKS

Aquinas, Thomas St., Doctor Angelicus, *Summa Theologiae,* cura et studio Sac. Petri Caramello, cum textu ex recensione Leonina, Taurini, Romae: Marietti, 1950.

Augustine, Charles, *A Commentary on the New Code of Canon Law,* 8 vols., 2. ed., St. Louis and London, 1918-1924.

Ayrinhac, H. A., Lydon, P., *Marriage Legislation in The New Code of Canon Law,* New York, 1932.

Barbosa, A., *Votorum Decisivorum, et Consultativorum Canonicorum, Libri* II, 2 vols. in 1, Lugduni, 1663-1664.

Benedictus XIV (Prospero Lambertini), *De Synodo Diocesana,* 4 vols., Mechliniae, 1842.

———, *Institutiones Ecclesiasticae, Latina* Venata, 2 vols., Venetiis, 1788.

———, *Opera Omnia,* 15 vols. in 7, Novissima ed., Venetiis, 1788.

Beste, Udalricus, *Introductio in Codicem,* 3. ed., Collegeville, Minnesota: St. John's Abbey Press, 1946.

Bouscaren, T. L., *Canon Law Digest,* 2 vols. and Supplement through 1948, Milwaukee, Wisc.: The Bruce Publishing Co., 1934—1943, 1949.

Bouscaren, T. L., Ellis A., *Canon Law, a Text and Commentary,* 2. ed., 2nd. printing, Milwaukee: Bruce, 1953.

Bowe, T. J., *Religious Superioresses,* The Catholic University of America Canon Law Studies, n. 228, Washington, D. C.: The Catholic University of America Press, 1946.

Brennan, James H., *Simple Convalidation of Marriage,* The Catholic University of America Canon Law Studies, n. 102, Washington, D. C.: The Catholic University of America, 1937.

Cappello, Felix, *Tractatus Canonico-Moralis de Sacramentis,* 5 vols., Vol. IV, *De Sacr. Ordindtione,* 3. ed., 1951, Vol. V, *De Matrimonio,* 6. ed., 1950, *Romae:* Marietti.

———, *Summa Iuris Canonici,* 3 vols., Vol. I, 5. ed., Romae: Apud Aedes Universitatis Gregerianae, 1951.

Carrière, Jos., *De Matrimonio,* 2. ed., Parisiis; Apud Mequignon Juniorem, 1842 (joined to De Justitia, 1854).

Chelodi, Ioannes-Ciprotti, Pius, *Ius Canonicum de Matrimonio et de Iudiciis Matrimonialibus,* 5. ed., Vicenza: Societa Anonima Tipografica Editrice, 1947.

Cicognani, Amleto, *Canon Law,* 2. ed., Philadelphia: Dalphin Press, 1935.

Claeys, Bouuaert F.-Simenon G., *Manuale Juris Canonici ad usum Seminariorum,* 3 vols., Vols. I et III, 5 ed., Vol. II, 3 ed., Gandae et Leodii, I, 1939; II, 1947; III, 1943.

Coronata, Mattheus Conte, *Tractatus de Sacramentis,* 3 vols., 2. ed., Taurini: Marietti, 1943-1946.

Davis, H., *Moral and Pastoral Theology,* 4 vols., 6. ed., London, New York: Sheed and Ward, Inc., 1949.

De Smet, A., *De Sponsalibus et Matrimonio,* 2 vols., 3 ed., Brugis: Car. Beyaert, 1920-1923, 4. ed., 1927.

Dillon, Robert E., *Common Law Marriage,* The Catholic University of America Canon Law Studies, n. 153, Washington, D. C.: The Catholic University of America Press, 1942.

Durand de Maillane, P. T., *Dictionnaire de Droit Canonique,* 2. ed., 4 vols., Lyons, 1770.

Eagleton, George B., *The Diocesan Quinquennial Faculties Formula IV,* The Catholic University of America Canon Law Studies, n. 248, Washington, D. C.: The Catholic University of America Press, 1948.

Esmein, A.-Genestal, R. Dauvillier, Jr., *Le Mariage en Droit Canonique,* 2 vols., Parisiis: Recueil Sirez, 1929-1935.

Fang, F., *Dispensatio Matrimonialis,* Romae: Officium Libri Catholici, 1946.

Feije, Henricus Joannes, *De Impedimentis et Dispensationibus Matrimonialibus,* 3. ed., Lovanii, 1885.

Garcia, F.-Bayon, J., *Tractatus Canonico-Moralis de Sacramento Matrimonii,* 2 vols., Madrid, 1931.

Gallagher, John F., *The Matrimonial Impediment of Public Propriety,* The Catholic University of America Canon Law Studies, n. 304, Washington, D. C.: The Catholic University of America Press, 1952.

Gasparri, Petrus, *Tractatus Canonicus de Matrimonio,* 2 vols., Nova ed., ad mentem Codicis, Romae: Typis Polyglottis Vaticanis, 1932.

———, *Tractatus Canonicus de Matrimonio,* 1. ed., 2 vols., Parisiis, 1891-1892.

———, *Tractatus Canonicus de Matrimonio,* 3. ed., 2 vols., Parisiis, 1904.

Génestal, R., *Histoire de La Legitimation des Enfants Naturels en Droit Canonique,* Parisiis, 1905.

Giovine, Petrus, *De Dispensationibus Matrimonialibus,* 2 vols., Neapoli, 1963.

Gonzalez Tellez, E., *Commentaria Perpetua in Singulos Textus Quinque Librorum Decretalium Gregorii IX,* 5 vols., Lugduni, 1673.

Gury, Joannes Petrus, *Compendium Theologiae Moralis,* Romana ed., ex Officina Typo-polyglotta S.C. de Propaganda Fide, Romae, 1872.

Gutierrez Ioannes, *Canonicae Quaestiones,* 3 vols. in 2, Lugduni, 1661.

Haile, Martin, *The Life of Reginald Pole,* New York, 1910.

Harrigan, Robert J., *The Radical Sanation of Invalid Marriages,* The Catholic University of America Canon Law Studies, n. 116, Washington, D. C.: The Catholic University of America, 1938.

Hostiensis, Cardinalis (Henricus de Segusio), *Commentaria in Quinque Decretalium* Libros, 5 vols., Venetiis, 1581.

Summe Aurea, Venetiis, 1570.

Hurtado, Thomas, *Tractatus de Sacramentis et Censuris, Lugduni,* 1666.

La Croix, Claudius, *Theologia Moralis,* 3 vols. in 2, Venetiis, 1747.

McCarthy, J., *The Matrimonial Impediment of Impotence With Special Reference to the Physical Capacity for Marriage of an "Excised Woman" and of a "Doubly Vasectomised" Man,* Romae, Catholic Book Agency, 1948.

McDevitt, Gilbert J., *Legitimacy and Legitimation,* The Catholic University of America Canon Law Studies, n. 138, Washington, D. C.: The Catholic University of America Press, 1941.

Martin, Jean Pierre, *De Matrimonio et Potestate Ipsum Dirimendi Ecclesiae Soli Exclusive Propria,* 2 vols., Lugduni, Parisiis: Apud Perisse Fratres, 1844.

Motry, Hubert L., *Diocesan Faculties According to the Code of Canon Law,* The Catholic University of America Canon Law Studies, n. 16, Washington, D. C.: The Catholic University of America, 1922.

Nau, Louis J., *Manual on the Marriage Laws of the Code of Canon Law,* New York-Cincinnati, 1933.

Noldin, H. Schmidt, A., *Summa Theologiae Moralis iuxta Codicem Iuris Canonici,* 3 vols., 27. ed., Ratisbone, Romae, Neo Eboraci: Pustet, 1940.

O'Keeffe, Gerard, M., *Matrimonial Dispensations, Powers of Bishops, Priests, and Confessors,* The Catholic University of America Canon Law Studies, n. 45, Washington, D. C.: The Catholic University of America, 1927.

O'Neill, William H., *Papal Rescripts of Favor,* The Catholic University of America Canon Law Studies, n. 57, Washington, D. C.: The Catholic University of America, 1930.

Panormitanus, Abbas (Nicholaus de Tudeschis), *Commentaria in Quinque Libros Decretalium,* 5 vols. in 7, Venetiis, 1588.

Palmieri, Dominicus, *Tractatus de Matrimonio Christiano,* Romae, 1880.

Payen, C., *De Matrimonio in Missionibus,* 2. ed., 3 vols., Zi-Ka-Wei, 1935-1936.

Perrone, Jr., *De Matrimonio Christiano,* 2d. ed., 3 vols., Vol. II, Leodii, 1861.

Petrovits, Joseph, *The New Church Law on Matrimony,* Philadelphia, 1921.

Pichler, Vitus, *Ius Canonicum Secundum Quinque Decretalium Titulos Gregorii IX,* 2 vols., Venetiis, 1741.

Pirhing, E., *Ius Canonicum in V Libros Decretalium Distributum,* 5 vols. in 4, Dilingae, 1674-1678.

Pontas, Joannes, *Dictionarium Casuum Conscientiae,* 3 vols., novissima ed., Venetiis: Bartoli, 1773.

Pyrrhus, Corradus, *Praxis Dispensationum Apostolicarum,* Neapoli, 1641.

Reiffenstuel, Annacletus, *Ius Canonicum Universum,* 5 vols. in 7, Parisiis, 1864-1870.

Rigantius, J. B., *Commentaria in Regulas, Constitutiones et Ordinationes Cancellariae Apostolicae,* 4 vols., Coloniae Allobrogum, 1751.

Rosset, Michael, *De Sacramento Matrimonii Tractatus Dogmaticus, Moralis, Liturgicus et Iudiciarius,* 6 vols., Parisiis, 1895-1896.

Sägmüeller, Johannes B., *Lehrbuch des katholischen Kirchenrechts,* 3 vols., Breisgau, 1904.

Sanchez, Thomas, *De Sancto Matrimonii Sacramento Disputationum Libri Tres,* 3 vols., Lugduni, 1669.

Scherer, Rudolf,-Ritter V., *Handbuch des Kirchenrechten,* 2 vols., Graz, 1886-1898.

Schmalzgrueber, Franciscus, *Ius Ecclesiasticum Universum,* 5 vols. in 12, Romae, 1843-1845.

Schenk, Francis J., *The Matrimonial Impediments of Mixed Religion and Disparity of Cult.* The Catholic University of America Canon Law Studies, n. 51, Washington, D. C.: The Catholic University of America, 1929.

Tanquerey, A., *Synopsis Theologiae Moralis,* 3 vols., Vol. III, 12. ed., 1943, Vols. I and II, 10. ed., Vol. I, 1925, Vol. II, 1937, New York: Benziger Bros.

Théphany, J. N., *Traité des Dispenses Matrimoniales,* Parisiis, 1889.

Van Espen, Bernardus, *Opera Omnia Canonica In Sex Partes distributa, Pars prima-tertia complectens Iuris Ecclesiastici Universi, Hodiernae Disciplinae praesertim Belgii, Galliae, Germaniae, & vincinarum Provinciarum accomodati. Primam Partem: cum additionibus, quae in supplemento extabant, suis locis diligenter insertis,* 6 vols. in 3, Lovanii, 1732.

Vermeersh, A.-Creusen, J., *Epitome Iuris Canonici,* 3 vols., Vol. II, 6. ed., Brugis: H. Dessain, 1940.

Vromant, G., *Ius Missionariorum,* 6 vols., Vol. V, *De Matrimonio,* Lovanii' Museum Lessianum, 1931.

Wahl, Francis X., *Consanguinity and Affinity,* The Catholic University of America Canon Law Studies, n. 90, Washington, D. C.: The Catholic University of America, 1934.

Wernz, Franciscus-Xav., *Ius Decretalium ad Usum Praelectionum in Scholis Textus Canonici Sive Iuris Decretalium,* 6 vols., Vol. IV, Romae, 1904.

Wernz, Franciscus-Vidal, Petrus, *Ius Canonicum ad Codicis Norman Exactum,* 7 vols. in 8, Vol. V, *Ius Matrimoniale,* 3. ed., Romae: Apud Aedes Universatis Gregorianae, 1946.

Woywod, S., *A Practical Commentary on the Code of Canon Law,* 2 vols., New York, 1925.

Zitelli, Z., *De Dispensationibus Matrimonialibus,* Romae, 1887.

Articles

Bastnagel, C. V., "Legitimate Status for High Dignities," *The Jurist,* VIII (1948), 219-222.

Bernhard, J., "Propos sur la Nature Juridique de la 'Sanatio in Radice' dans le Droit Canonique Actuel," *Ephemerides Iuris Canonici,* IV (1948), 389-406.

———, "L'Explication Juridique de la Retroactivité de la 'Sanatio in Radice' dans la Doctrine Canonique Moderne," *Ephemerides Iuris Canonici,* VII (1951), 80-88.

———, "La 'Sanatio in Radice' et la Legitimation des Enfants, dans la Doctrine Canonique Moderne," *Revue de Droit Canonique,* II (1952), 30-56.

Ciprotti, P., "De Prole Legitima vel Illegitima in Iure Canonico Vigenti," Apolli*naris,* XII (1939), 329-347; 490-519.

Periodicals

Apollinaris, Romae, 1928—.

Ephemerides Iuris Canonici, Romae, 1945—.

Jurist, The, Washington, 1941—.

Revue de Droit Canonique, Strasbourg, 1951—

Abbreviations

AAS—*Acta Apostolicae Sedis.*
ASS—*Acta Sanctae Sedis.*
C.—Caput; causa.
Can.—Canon.
D.—Digesta.
Inst.—*Institutiones.*
MGH—*Monumenta Germaniae Historica.*
N.—Numero.
Q.—Quaestio.
S.C. de Prop. Fide—Sacra Congregatio de Propaganda Fide.

ALPHABETICAL INDEX

BIOGRAPHICAL NOTE

THOMAS CHARLES RYAN was born September 2, 1924, in Phillipsburg, New Jersey. He received his elementary and secondary education in Sts. Philip and James Grammar School and High School in Phillipsburg. After graduating from high school, he attended St. Charles' College in Catonsville, Maryland, graduating from that institution on June 6, 1944. The same year he entered Immaculate Conception Seminary in Darlington, New Jersey. In this seminary he received his education in philosophy and theology prior to his ordination to the Sacred Priesthood. He was ordained to the priesthood on June 3, 1950, by His Excellency, George W. Ahr, Bishop of Trenton. He served as a parochial curate in St. James' Parish, Woodbridge, and St. Peter's Parish, New Brunswick, New Jersey. He enrolled in the School of Canon Law at the Catholic University of America in October, 1951, and received the degree of Bachelor of Canon Law in June, 1952, and of Licentiate in Canon Law in June, 1953.

CANON LAW STUDIES*

349. Bottoms, Rev. Archibald M., J.C.L., The discretionary authority of the ecclesiastical judge in matrimonial trials of the first instance.
350. Kekumano, Rev. Charles A., A.B., J.C.L., The secret archives of the diocesan curia.
351. McGrath, Rev. Robert Eamon, O.M.I., J.C.L., The local superior in non-exempt clerical congregations.
352. McManus, Rev. Frederick Richard, A.B., J.C.L., The Congregation of Sacred Rites.
353. Rodimer, Rev. Frank J., A.B., S.T.L., J.C.L., The canonical effects of infamy of fact.
354. Rouillard, Rev. Jacques, A.B., Ph.B., J.C.L., Une étude comparés du droit canonique et du droit civil paroissal de la Province de Kuébec dans l'administration des biens paroissaux.
355. Ryan, Rev. Thomas C., J.C.L., The juridical effects of the *sanatio in radice*.
356. Sullivan, Rev. Bernard Owens, J.C.L., Legislation and requirements for permissible cohabitation in invalid marriages
357. Tatarczuk, Rev. Vincent Anthony, A.B., S.T.L., J.C.L., Infamy of law.

* For a complete list of the available numbers of this series apply to the Catholic University of America Press, 620 Michigan Ave., N. E., Washington (17), D. C.

www.ingramcontent.com/pod-product-compliance
Lightning Source LLC
LaVergne TN
LVHW050215080826
844660LV00012B/416

* 9 7 8 0 8 1 3 2 2 5 2 2 7 *